ENTERPRISE CONTENT MANAGEMENT
A Business and Technical Guide

Stephen A. Cameron

bcs

The
Chartered
Institute
for IT

Published by British Informatics Society Limited (BISL), a wholly owned subsidiary of BCS The Chartered Institute for IT First Floor, Block D, North Star House, North Star Avenue, Swindon, SN2 1FA, UK. www.bcs.org

ISBN 978-1-906124-67-0

British Cataloguing in Publication Data.
A CIP catalogue record for this book is available at the British Library.

Typeset by The Charlesworth Group.
Printed by Charlesworth Press.

To Martine

CONTENTS

LIST OF FIGURES AND TABLES

ABOUT THE AUTHOR

Stephen Cameron has wide experience of information management systems, gained over more than 30 years in a variety of organisations. These include Syntegra, Post Office, Marconi Communications, IBM Informix, Xansa, Aon and BearingPoint.

Stephen attended the Duke of York's Royal Military School, before studying for an honours degree in Electrical and Electronic Engineering at Brunel University whilst being a sponsored student apprentice at Marconi Communications in Chelmsford.

During his work and studies, he built and coded a number of operating systems and microprocessor emulators. While working in technical authorship in the computing system laboratories at Writtle, the author worked on System X telephony and message switch exchanges.

He published his first journal article in Electronics and Wireless World in the mid-80s during his studies. Discovering databases he developed a language de-compiler, created several user groups and launched a service to recover lost source code.

Stephen moved into consulting practice leading to participating in BS and ANSI database standards. Having thoroughly mastered structured information systems, he then took on the challenges of the unstructured world of content and process management, working since the late 90's on content management solutions including extensible database technologies such as GIS systems.

His recent academic interest involves innovation development practices and information philosophy. His other ventures include being a magician, beekeeper, potter, comedy writer and tennis player.

FOREWORD

... 70% ... 80% ... 90% ... content matters.

Common wisdom suggests unstructured information constitutes 70–90% of an organisation's total. It is also widely acknowledged that the majority of that unstructured information is not managed. But does ECM matter? Surely our world strives to be paperless.

This eternal myth continues to present a target for which organisations struggle to have an appetite, let alone any realistic strategy. Of course, this doesn't really address the issue at hand: the science and the art of unstructured information have long been less about the digitisation of paper and much more about managing an increasing variety of information types.

Information is the real intellectual property of an organisation. It is one of the three key types of asset, alongside money and people, that an organisation has to juggle with as it strives to understand its markets, citizens, risks and everyday decisions. So, as a key asset, it should be exploited as fully as possible. Yet it isn't. Information is treated as a second-class citizen. For the most part it is created as a corollary of the activities that we and our systems perform. Stephen refers to the flotsam of events and perspectives and the need to manage the jetsam of time: a good analogy and an opportunity lost.

So ECM does matter. Content – unstructured information – is special. To collect, store, understand, describe, share and manage it throughout its life requires particular technologies. Focus is being applied to bringing as much of the flotsam and jetsam under some order as possible: ensuring that organisations identify what is important to keep and what can be discarded. Furthermore organisations understand that this stuff costs. The burden of administration is huge and a technology that has been at best unwieldy, making it difficult to implement, and which, when deployed, can have such an impact on an organisation's culture, has been confined to departmental silos but is now being socialised, perhaps even commoditised. In so doing that lost opportunity may at last be realised.

The next wave of capability will allow for real exploitation of unstructured information. It will introduce the ability to analyse deeply all of the content in order to identify and action patterns and resolve complex problems. Initially the focus will be on the user, but increasingly this will be automated, combining both unstructured and structured information to truly inform decisions and initiate events.

In the future content will not be special. After all, we take decisions based on the information before us, irrespective of form or type. Increasingly organisations will look for common ways to organise, describe and execute policy around all of their information. Information will be trusted: we will understand the lineage of its processing and be able to traverse huge information sets because of the automated classification and relationships created during acquisition and usage. Information will be delivered so, rather than fishing in the dark, a.k.a. searching, a trusted view of contextual information will be pushed – not pulled – to the decision point.

Books handling these topics to the right level of depth from both business and technical viewpoints within one volume are, in my opinion, very rare. Stephen has created a unique perspective for both audiences, providing insight and guidance that will allow better understanding of the requirements and constraints that surround enterprise content management. I have worked with Stephen since the late '90s and he has always brought a style and passion to every project that is strangely compelling: you always want to hear more. This book is no exception.

It is so easy to consider the next item that arrives in the inbox as critical. But, as a good friend of mine once counselled me, 'Stop doing what is urgent and focus on what is important'. Information is important.

Douglas Coombs
Lead Consultant, Information and Process (North East Europe)
IBM Corporation

GLOSSARY

The glossary has been collated from various sources including AIIM, Intellect and from the Mike2.0 methodology mike2.openmethodology.org/wiki/ ECM_Maturity_Model_(ecm3) *made available under the Creative Commons Attribution License.*

AIIM Formerly the Association for Information and Image Management, now just AIIM. Originally formed to provide education, professional development and standards for microfilm and electronic image processing, its scope has expanded to include the enterprise content management (ECM) industry. It is an ANSI/ISO-accredited standards development enterprise.

ANSI American National Standards Institute. Private US Agency that co-ordinates the development and maintenance of various industry standards.

API Application Programming Interface: the specific method prescribed by a program by which a programmer can make requests of it.

Application server A server program which houses the business logic for an application. Application servers, or 'app servers', execute operations to complete transactions and other interactions between end-users and a business's back-end databases and applications. They provide functionality such as clustering, database access classes, transaction processing and messaging. For tiered applications, best practice calls for this application processing to be separated from the actual retrieval of web pages, which is done by a web server operating in front of the app server.

Archive A collection of computer files that have been packaged together for backup. This is done so that they can be transported to some other location and saved away from the computer so that more hard disk storage space can be made available, or for some other purpose. An archive can include a simple list of files, or files organised under a directory or catalogue structure (depending on how a particular program supports archiving).

ARMA The Association of Records Managers and Administrators.

Browser The distribution platform for internet-based applications. These can interpret the presentation of standards in HTML slightly differently. Applications that are immune to those different interpretations should therefore have to be created. These would either have to keep to core simple page rendering or manage the differences between browsers' interpretations.

Business Process Management (BPM) A mix of process management and workflows with application integration technology.

Categorisation Organising documents and other content into logical groupings, based on their contents.

Certification The process of issuing of a formal statement confirming the results of an evaluation, and that the evaluation criteria used were correctly applied.

Classification A method of assigning retention and disposition rules to records. Similar to the 'declare' function, this can be a completely manual process or a process-driven one, depending on the particular implementation. As a minimum the user can be presented with a list of allowable file codes from a drop-down list (manual classification). Ideally the desktop process or application can automate classification by triggering a file code selection from one of its own properties or characteristics.

Cloud Computing Cloud computing is made possible by the establishment of virtual private networks (VPNs) that can be used and accessed by the organisation to serve its customers.

Compound Document A document that may contain components from other documents and information sources.

Computer Output to Laser Disk (COLD) Term often used interchangeably with 'ERM'.

Content Management Interoperability Services (CMISs) A specification for utilising web services and Web 2.0 interfaces to enable interoperability of content management repositories from different vendors.

Controlled Vocabularies An organised list of words, phrases, or some other set of labels employed to identify and retrieve documents. A collection of preferred terms that are used to assist in more precise retrieval of content. Controlled vocabulary terms can be used for populating attribute values when indexing, building labelling systems, and creating style guides and database schemata. One type of controlled vocabulary is the thesaurus.

Corpus A complete collection of objects.

Darwin Information Typing Architecture (DITA) An XML-based architecture for authoring, producing, and delivering information. Although its main applications have so far been in technical publications, DITA is also used for other types of documents such as policies, procedures, and training.

Declare Designate a particular document as a corporate record.

Digital Asset Management (DAM) A practice enabling enterprises to organise and repurpose media assets to streamline costs and enhance revenues. DAM systems are especially suited to managing multimedia content, and tend to offer hooks into specialised desktop media authoring systems.

Disposition What is done with records that are no longer needed for current business. Disposition possibilities include transferring records, destroying temporary records, and transferring records of continuing value to archives.

Document A written paper, recording, photograph, computer file, or other item that bears the original, official, or legal form of something and can be used to furnish evidence or information. A document can be a single page or a collection of pages that constitute a report. A record is a document.

Document Management Software that controls and organises documents throughout an enterprise. Incorporates document and content capture, workflow, document repositories, COLD/ERM and output systems, and information retrieval systems. The method for sharing content and instilling version control. In the document lifecycle, document management manages the creation or inception of a document, whilst records management deals fundamentally with the document at the end of its lifecycle as it becomes published.

Document Repository Site where source documents or other content objects are stored.

DoD 5015.2 United States Department of Defence (DoD), Design Criteria Standard for Electronic Records Management Software Applications.

Dublin Core Metadata Initiative (DCMI) An enterprise promoting the adoption of interoperable metadata standards and the development of specialised metadata vocabularies for describing resources that enable more intelligent information discovery systems. A core set of accepted metadata fields is known as 'the Dublin Core'.

Electronic Document Management System (EDMS) A traditional and still commonly used term describing ECM systems, though usually those with a focus on imaging, document management and workflows.

Electronic Reports Management (ERM) A technology that ingests print stream data, stores and indexes it, and then makes it available in report form on demand to end-users.

Enterprise Content Management (ECM) A generic industry term for software products that manage unstructured data such as documents, images, files and web content.

Federated Records Management Allows organisations to enforce records retention rules across multiple disparate repositories.

File Plans A common classification scheme for the entire enterprise. The file plan is typically a hierarchical set of subjects or business activities. Each node or subject file is annotated with a unique code called a file code. A given file code thus refers to a specific subject file within the file plan. Each subject file has an official retention rule – when, why and how to delete – assigned to it. Each record must be assigned a file code that matches the subject file within the file plan. This way documents with similar subjects are all assigned the appropriate retention rule.

Folksonomy A user-generated set of tags or categories: essentially the social software trend's answer to the taxonomy. Folksonomic tagging is intended to make a body of content easier to search, discover, and navigate. Folksonomy functionality is not inherent to most ECM suites. Folksonomies tend to arise in web-based communities where special provisions are made on the website for users to create and use tags.

Index List List containing data or metadata indicating the identity and location of a given file or document.

Integrative Document and Content Management (IDCM) Another term for ECM that is generally used much less, but is common in some parts of the world.

Intelligent Character Recognition (ICR) A form of OCR that includes the electronic intelligence to place captured document characters in a relevant context.

International Organization for Standardization (ISO) A worldwide federation of national standards bodies from some 100 countries, one from each country, founded in 1947. Among the standards it fosters is Open Systems Interconnection (OSI), a universal reference model for communication protocols.

Internet A network infrastructure which allows communication using a standard protocol between servers and nodes around the world. It uses the digital infrastructure on which telecommunications companies around the world base their systems. Virtual private networks can be created through the telecommunications company using its base infrastructure and creating a virtual and protected internet environment.

Intranet An internet bounded by the organisation. The web servers that provide web applications are only available to users within the organisation.

ISO 15489 Defines what a records management program should look like and provides best practice for how to develop and maintain a records management program.

Keyword search Search which compares an inputted word against an index and returns matching results.

Localisation The process of adapting a software product or service for different languages, countries, or cultures. In addition to language considerations, such as support for foreign character sets, localisation may require adaptations for currencies, time zones, national holidays, cultural assumptions and sensitivities, dialects, colour schemes, and general design conventions.

Metadata A definition or description of data, often described as data about data. For example the data of a newspaper story are the headline and the story, whereas the metadata describe who wrote it, when and where it was published, and what section of the newspaper it appeared in. Metadata can help us determine who content is for and where, how, and when it should appear. For documents published online, important metadata elements include the author's name, the title, the date of publication and the subject area.

Meta Tag An HTML command located within the header of a website that displays additional or referential data not present on the page itself.

Model Requirements for the Management of Electronic Records (MoReq2) A generic functional specification for systems designed to manage electronic records.

Official record A record that is legally recognised and has the judicially enforceable quality of being able to establish the information it contains as fact. In many cases it can be the original document.

Open Document Management API (ODMA) An open industry standard that enables desktop applications to interface with a document management system (DMS). ODMA simplifies cross-platform and cross-application file communication by standardising access to document management through an API. ODMA allows multiple applications to access the same DMS without the need for a hard-coded link.

Optical Character Recognition (OCR) Technology that recognises alphanumeric characters in fixed form – for example on a scanned paper document – and captures and digitises them.

Organization for the Advancement of Structured Information Standards (OASIS) A not-for-profit consortium that drives the development, convergence and adoption of open standards for the global information society.

Original Equipment Manufacturer Manufacturer whose products or components are purchased and rebranded by another company.

PDF/A A joint activity between NPES – the Association for Suppliers of Printing, Publishing and Converting Technologies – and AIIM International to develop an international standard that defines the use of the Portable Document Format (PDF) for archiving and preserving documents.

Records Any documentary material, regardless of physical form or characteristics, made or received by an enterprise in pursuance of law or in connection with the transaction of business, and used by that enterprise or its successor as evidence of activities or because of informational value.

Records Management (RM) A professional discipline primarily concerned with the management of document-based information systems. The application of systematic and scientific controls to recorded information required in the operation of an organisation's business. The systematic control of all organisational records during the various stages of their lifecycle: from their creation or receipt, through their processing, distribution, maintenance and use, to their ultimate disposition. The purpose of records management is to promote economies and efficiencies in record keeping, to ensure that useless records are systematically destroyed while valuable information is protected and maintained in a manner that facilitates its use.

Records Retention Policy A plan for the management of records listing types of record and how long they should be kept. The purpose is to provide the continuing authority to dispose of or transfer records.

Relational Database Management System (RDBMS) A collection of programs that allows the creation, storage, modification and administration of a relational database. An RDBMS stores data in related tables, and information can be extracted from the database through structured query language (SQL) statements. Because the data in a relational system are spread across tables, rather than housed in a flat file, the same database can be viewed in many different ways. Almost all complex databases today use an RDBMS, including most business databases.

Repository Part of a document or content management system. Its specific function is to control the checking in and out of material, version control, and look-up against defined attributes.

Representational State Transfer (REST) Software architecture for distributed internet systems. Specifically it is an alternative to web services and SOAP for integrating services and repositories without requiring messaging or cookies.

Retention Period The period of time during which records must be retained in a certain location or form. A retention period may be stated in terms of months or years, and is sometimes contingent upon the occurrence of an event.

Retention Schedules Records retention schedules are lists and descriptions of public records. They include information about how long each type of record should be kept (retention period) and what should happen to it at the end of that period (disposition).

Rich Internet Application (RIA) A web application that has the functionality and features of traditional desktop applications. Typically the applications transfer necessary functions to the client – in this case the web browser – which removes the need for a page to refresh every time a new piece of information is needed. While RIAs run in a web browser, they don't usually require software installation.

Service Oriented Architecture (SOA) A collection of services that connect with each other to perform a function or activity. This gives the human interface portion of an application more independence from the data processing activity.

Simple Object Access Protocol (SOAP) The predominant standard protocol in the web Services family. It is an XML construct that allows applications to be invoked remotely and deliver information back to the calling service.

Structured data Data that can be represented according to specific descriptive parameters, for example rows and columns, in a relational database, or hierarchical nodes, in an XML document or fragment.

Taxonomy In science, taxonomy allows people to precisely identify any organism by its kingdom, phylum, class, order, family, genus and species. It does the same job within content management: it describes a classification structure for content. This structure, typically highly regimented, affects the data model, directory structure, and file naming conventions for a given implementation of a content management system. In more complex scenarios taxonomies are often multifaceted, meaning multiple hierarchies or categorisation trees may be used to classify content. This allows users to find content via more than one path or hierarchy. As an example, one might find information about red rock crabs via a biology facet under animals/invertebrates/crustaceans, while another might find one via a geography facet under world/land/Australasia. Taxonomy can also be language-oriented, as in specifications for subsets of XML such as ebXML.

Thesaurus A collection of words in a cross-referencing system that refers to multiple taxonomies and provides a kind of meta-classification, thereby facilitating document retrieval.

Unstructured information Information that is without document or data structure, i.e. cannot be effectively decomposed into constituent elements or chunks for atomic storage and management.

Vital records Records that contain unique or irreplaceable information and require special protection. These include articles of incorporation, annual reports and shareholder records

Web Content Management (WCM) A component of ECM which specialises in the management of content for presentation specifically through browsers. The management of a site's content and its configuration for presentation is typically provided through the same browser web channel. ECM collaboration controls and tools may also be presented and controlled through WCM.

Web Services A set of standards to support application interoperability over the HTTP protocol.

Workflow Automation of business processes, in whole or in part, where documents, information or tasks are passed from one participant to another for action, according to a set of rules. A business process is a logically related set of workflows, work steps, and tasks that provides a product or service to customers.

XML (Extensible Mark-up Language) An established standard, based on the Standard Generalized Mark-up Language, designed to facilitate document construction from standard data items. XML is also used as a generic data exchange mechanism. Since XML describes the underlying information and its structure, content can be separated from look and feel. This overcomes a severe limitation of formatted word processing or HTML documents, which merely describe content presentation for a particular set of compliant applications (like web browsers).

PREFACE

Information is the lifeblood of knowledge, the flotsam of events and perspectives created in every second of history. There is so much to capture and yet so little time and so few resources to make sense of it all. Just as we get tantalisingly close, the holy grail of true knowledge slips further over the horizon.

To capture this jetsam of time, to find some meaning and to predict the future is an eternal struggle. We take our experience about the world and transform it into a repository of knowledge that will sustain beyond our own lifetime. It is a quest for recognition.

The pursuit of the perfect representation of knowledge is all-encompassing, applicable at any time, multifaceted and understood by all. It is the yoke of our endeavour that we aim for all these ideals.

In order to achieve clarity we must clear our minds of the clutter and pretence of the everyday and balance our thoughts with the contributions of others to direct and consider our machinations. There is a dichotomy: single-mindedness must be carefully balanced with the creative vigour of the team.

This book aims to define the enterprise content management (ECM) approach to developing the organisational repository of knowledge, and achieve clarity in the midst of a multiplicity of global viewpoints. This book is not an encyclopaedia on ECM, because to do so would be to write about every aspect of information management: there are online tools that satisfy that need. I hope to give the reader a strong sense of purpose about content in the enterprise: how it affects and is affected by the organisation and its processes. This book tries to be agnostic about products, solutions and technology.

This book could not have been completed without help from industry leaders in ECM. I count among them Doug Coombs, who kindly wrote the foreword, and AIIM, who gave me the opportunity to meet many customers and vendors over the last 10 years. I also thank Matthew Flynn for his gentle yet insistent encouragement, and the members of BCS's north London branch: Dalim Basu, Richard Tandoh and Jude Umeh. To all those who have inspired me on the way: Pat Hannon, for his extraordinary gift for engineering, Mark Burnett, for his inspiring methods using SouthBeach, Jonathan Barber, Mike Brakes, Nick Carus, Carl Chilley, Ray Fielding, Lisa Gibbard and Ben Kahn, for being sage mirrors, mentors and alternative thinkers and influencers throughout my work.

No book would be complete without a complementary internet presence.
This book forms the high level milestone on the background to ECM thinking.
There is, however, constant change on the road to ECM: suppliers, products
and technology. All of these areas are captured at www.ecmguide.org
where there is also an opportunity to ask questions and provide answers.

STRUCTURE

BUSINESS AND TECHNICAL PERSPECTIVES

This book is split into two halves: business and technical guides. The business guide provides the business prerequisites for establishing ECM, whilst the technical guide outlines the delivery aspects.

For each concept introduced in the business guide an equivalent delivery-focused discussion takes part in the technical guide.

Figure 0.1 Business and technical comparable perspectives

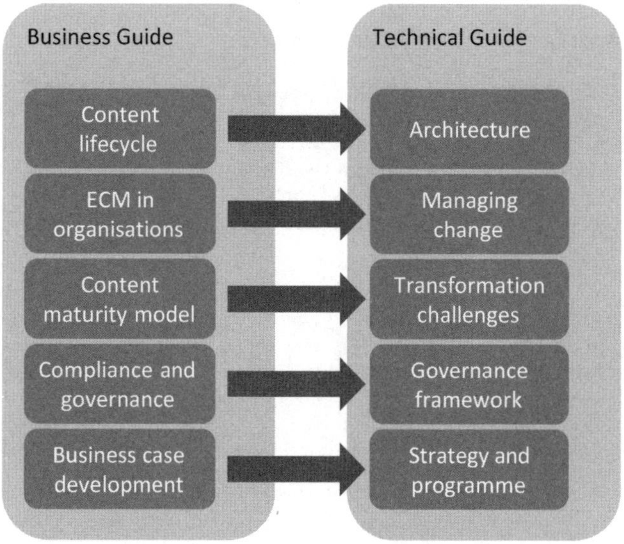

The business guide introduces the ECM lifecycle, describes how organisations work with information, introduces the concept of a maturity model for content, and discusses the areas of compliance affecting organisations. Finally it provides a breakdown of the specialist areas to address in the creation of a business case.

The technical guide provides an open discussion of the architectural frameworks which can be adopted, selecting those appropriate to ECM. It describes methods and tools for managing change in the organisation and charts the progression through the content maturity model. It also details how to implement the governance and compliance framework, and lists anomalies and issues which arise when developing strategies and delivering programmes.

Finally a future trends chapter discusses some of the technologies in the architectural framework which are likely to change or improve. A glossary collates and discusses in a single place the ECM components mentioned throughout.

PROJECT LIFECYCLE PERSPECTIVE

There is a straightforward business mantra on strategy used before starting any new work: 'Know where you are, find out where you want to go and plan how to get there.'

In a similar way the structure of the chapters may be used to develop a strategy through a similar three step process: assessment, business case and delivery.

Figure 0.2 The project lifecycle

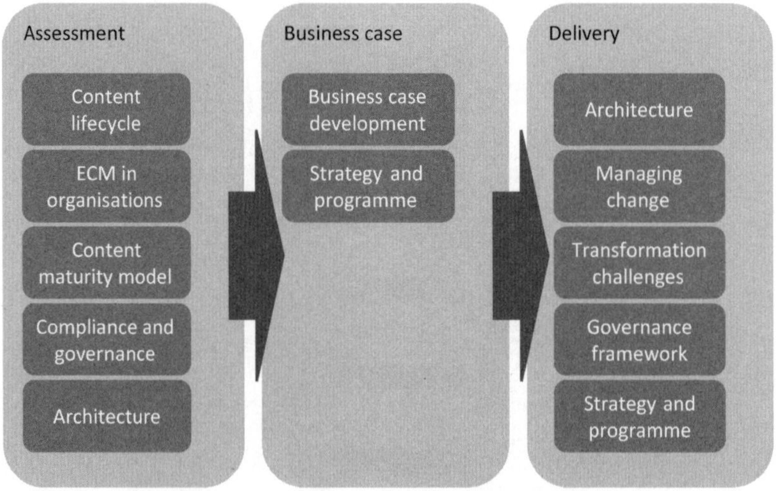

Assessment
- Content lifecycle
- ECM in organisations
- Content maturity model
- Compliance and governance
- Architecture

Business case
- Business case development
- Strategy and programme

Delivery
- Architecture
- Managing change
- Transformation challenges
- Governance framework
- Strategy and programme

PART 1: ECM BUSINESS GUIDE

This business guide aims to:

(i)   introduce ECM;

(ii)   describe the information lifecycle and methods for valuing content for key performance indicators (KPIs);

(iii)   establish how organisations use ECM;

(iv)   define an ECM maturity model to gauge an organisation's current and future ECM use;

(v)   illustrate where ECM can address compliance and governance;

(vi)   build a business case with measures for success when adopting ECM.

INTRODUCTION

I keep six honest serving-men
They taught me all I knew;
Their names are What and Why and When
And How and Where and Who
Rudyard Kipling

DEFINITION OF ECM

The simplest definition of enterprise content management (ECM) is the management of information in all its forms across an organisation. This aims to capture, preserve and deliver information as a corporate asset in a consistent, natural and re-usable way, so that an organisation can sustain, enhance and tune its knowledge investment.

Apart from this management, ECM refers to the related strategies, methods and tools. ECM tools and strategies allow the management of an organisation's unstructured information, wherever and whenever this exists.

ECM is a strategy and methodology. Its name is a self-descriptive acronym with three overlapping concepts, as shown in Figure 0.3:

Figure 0.3 The scope of ECM

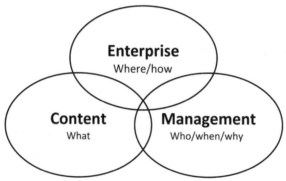

- The **enterprise** perspective describes all the functions of distribution, application, publication, acquisition, capture and access in a uniform and pervasive nature without boundaries. It defines where and how ECM takes effect.

- The **content** describes all the rich components, information, data (structured or unstructured), records, rules, structures, topics and templates. It defines what makes up ECM.

- The **management** discipline brings together facets of communication, processes, workflows, collaboration, interaction and exchange with a plethora of stakeholders. It describes who is involved in ECM, and why and when they interact.

A SHORT HISTORY OF ECM

ECM is a mature concept brimming with international standards and best practices garnered over 30 years. Its evolution matches changes in information technology and business needs.

It has developed on the back of technical and business conditions. First, the fact that paper could not easily be distributed to multiple parties without reproductive effort and cost. Second, the fact that computers were able to store scanned images of paper and distribute them relatively cheaply.

After some years, the document management perspective changed to reflect two trends. These were the substitution of electronic documents and media for paper and the use of the internet as a publishing medium.

Over time ECM evolved to encompass business process management, to aid the management and distribution of information. It also increasingly included internet-based collaborative environments. These allow users to compile and create content in a secure and regulated manner, and distribute it pervasively.

THE FUTURE OF ECM

In the future ECM aims to:

- ensure that repositories of the internet and organisations become federated, consistently searchable, shareable, verifiable and persistent sources;

- coalesce ideas into actionable, valuable knowledge through collaboration;

- protect organisations' ideas whilst sharing and fostering those appropriate for development in the public domain.

The internet has created both cohesion and fragmentation. It has made the globe smaller, breaking down old organisational walls by using a common protocol. In the new world there are no boundaries of country, race, class, gender, religion or government.

Primarily due to its omnipresence, the internet has become a font of knowledge and interaction. However those who use it become aware of its weaknesses. These include unverified sources, and ineffective and unfocused search results. It is unstructured, insecure and uncontrollable.

Figure 0.4 People, organisations and the internet

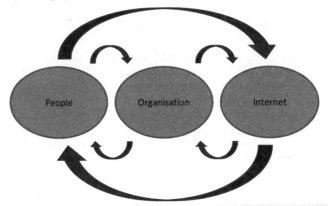

Organisations cannot have such weaknesses as they are guided by good corporate practice to be transparent. Their sources must be auditable and they have a duty of accuracy to their stakeholders.

Organisations need to have accurate information to make decisions, not the fuzzy information which is too often a part of the internet. Those that understand the value of their information, maintain their verifiable sources, work to share their ideas, create business propositions and protect their knowledge, whilst balancing this protection with the need to engage, will succeed.

Organisations are fertile ground for managing change and innovation. They are often the creators of new applications embraced by the internet.

ECM helps organisations to understand how to use powerful collaborative content structures that are the backbone of the internet, but without any loss of control.

The challenge of the information society is that the idealistic goals for true knowledge repositories and automated collaborative idea brokers are as yet unattainable.

An organisation which adopts ECM is in a privileged position to move into an emerging world where information and repositories become altruistically part of the greater internet community, but only when the time is right and the mechanisms are in place for the organisation to remain viable.

SUMMARY

ECM is a self-evident acronym which promotes pervasive, rich and interactive information management for an organisation. It is a mature concept which has evolved to match information technology and business needs. It has the potential to bring an organisation all the benefits of the pervasive, collaborative and rich content which has made the internet such a success.

1 CONTENT LIFECYCLE

Reporting is a cycle: No matter how much you work at sending a message, it's only successful if it's received
Jessica Savitch

ECM encompasses a number of strategies, methods and tools used to capture, manage, store, preserve and deliver content. It delivers the management of an organisation's unstructured information, wherever this exists.

Central to the basic model presented in an earlier chapter is the heart of the ECM process, the content lifecycle (please see Figure 1.1). This involves managing the acquisition, storage and delivery of content across the organisation. All these components have enterprise, content and management factors.

Figure 1.1 The content lifecycle

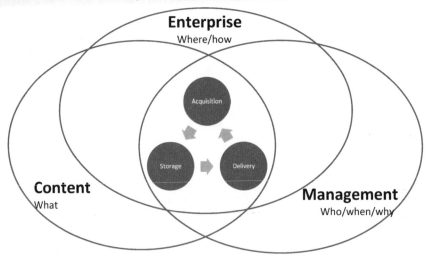

This process is known as the information lifecycle because the platforms and circumstances on which content is acquired or initiated are often the mechanisms from which it is delivered. The desktop, internet or multi-functional devices (combined fax/email/printer/scanner) are all examples. As television journalist Jessica Savitch once put it, the link between delivery and acquisition is a mark of success in developing news content.

In this chapter the lowest common denominator of content will be referred to as the content object.

Let us now look at each of these three areas: acquisition, storage and delivery.

ECM ACQUISITION

The mechanisms for acquisition include scanning, transformation, online submission and capture. This can be broken down into elements aligned to ECM within the lifecycle.

Enterprise acquisition

The enterprise may have a central capture repository to balance the performance and storage for its dispersed acquisition mechanisms. Traditional acquisition may be facilitated through the corporate desktop, which generates documents, the internet, which captures material submitted through web applications, or the scanning of documents using large scanning centres for bulk scanning and indexing. Enterprise acquisition can also be realised through scanning using MFDs (multi-functional devices) which can use an email system to distribute images or a central shared file store on which to deposit them. These can be accessed later by the people who understand the context of the content – an important factor in its successful cataloguing or indexing.

Content acquisition

Content can be acquired in various forms as it is collected and catalogued. This includes its original format, whether this is paper or electronic. Where it is not in its original form, it is transformed at the point of capture into enterprise agreed formats which can be stored universally,accepted and viewed.

Acquisition management

Capture management establishes the mechanism by which content is catalogued using skilled resources distributed throughout the organisation. This consists of a bulk transfer resource unit which carries out bulk-scan and cataloguing to a set protocol or indexing rule-set. These are typically supplemented by an electronic application form on which categorisation information can be entered to help find the content again.

Management recognises that review can improve the acquisition transformation. Together with workflow, as content is created, its indexing attributes also acquire clear and complete references. When content is first acquired or created, the threshold in terms of indexing or cataloguing for accepting it into the system is low. As it emerges through review it acquires a baseline index that is enhanced with clearer attributes and context which enrich it.

ECM STORAGE

ECM is not exclusively about the electronic mechanisms for storage. Let us look at the elements of the storage part of the lifecycle.

Enterprise storage

The enterprise characteristics of a repository can be distributed, federated or virtually delivered through a cloud. There are tools to manage access to virtual storage and large storage service facilities (often known as storage farms). The enterprise repository can be anything from a warehouse with shelves for the storage of original documents through to electronic images stored on a remote file store accessible over the internet.

Content storage

The content characteristic determines the mechanism by which an object is stored: whether it is transformed or disseminated into elements. It may also include a number of versions of the object, review attachments or object overlays to capture the transition or change in the object.

Storage management

Storage management uses process management to establish versions of content, control who has authorship rights and distribute content to those nominated to review. In the long term it may incorporate digital rights protection to ensure that content is encapsulated and protected from amendment or watermarked with ownership information. In the technical sphere it may include tools to extend storage capacity or manage the retention life of content, so that it can be destroyed correctly and at the right time.

ECM DELIVERY

The mechanisms for delivery include searching and publishing. Searching is considered a delivery mechanism for content because it is simply a mechanism for not delivering all the information at once.

Enterprise delivery

The internet infrastructure by which applications can be delivered universally to browsers provides a rich vein of options for distributing information. Mechanisms now exist for distributed publishing at point of sale or the efficient manufacture of specialist media in bulk. Each business will cost the specific mechanism which can be made available and set criteria by which content can be distributed via that channel.

Many content management systems start by managing content which is delivered for a single department: for example a marketing, financial reporting or claims department.

Content delivery

Information can be presented on the web page, encapsulated in downloadable electronic documents or provided in print. Each piece of content may be contained wholly within the repository or automatically constructed to form the basis of the delivery.

Delivery management

Managing delivery includes search technology: the means by which users can search for content to be published or presented as quickly as is practicable. Workflow or business process management (BPM) provides the mechanism for managing the delivery of objects used in the work between editors or users.

By addressing each of these nine areas derived from the components and defining the resources and mechanisms used for each, a successful ECM delivery is possible.

THE HISTORY OF INFORMATION CONSUMPTION

Society has changed from being a consumer to a generator of content. In the 1960s, as television reached the masses, there was an unquenchable thirst to consume information and content, with very few producers of content able to satiate this desire. In the 1990s the burgeoning use of the internet demanded more content. By 2010 content was being produced at a formidable rate, with a relatively small handful of consumption channels: YouTube, Facebook and Twitter.

Whilst society has changed the way it works with content, organisations have managed the transformation slowly. They have encouraged their personnel to create high-value content so that corporate decisions can be made quickly and authoritatively. The challenges that organisations face are linked to questions about how information can best be re-used or made more pervasive. Organisations decided to adopt the pervasive channels used by society. The downside is that these mechanisms rely on making interaction fun, creating a need to provide outlets for leisurely consumption of content. Organisations must consider the right balance of consumption and generation in their workplaces if they are to take advantage of mechanisms which work well over the internet.

Collaboration

Collaboration technologies were developed as a means by which external parties are encouraged to work and generate solutions to problems existing inside organisations. Collaboration can take several significant forms: wikis, policy derivation, forums, support, project management and meetings are a few examples. From the organisation's perspective they are geared to managing the involvement of stakeholders.

Collaboration requires an extensive reach to a number of stakeholders. The content which is used in collaboration needs to be pervasive across the organisation.

CASE STUDY: WIKILEAKS

WikiLeaks was founded in 2007. It anonymously acquires and publishes ethical, political and historical information to subvert international governments' communications from distorting analysis.

It exists due to failure and opportunity. There was concern that governments failed to provide correct and referential evidence for the presence of weapons of mass destruction in Iraq, which served as the prime reason for the war in 2003. Access to information had also been made easier by the conglomeration of US government analysis personnel in a number of government departments as a reaction to this failing. The governments involved recognised their failure to act on or co-ordinate disparate and non-shared analysis that could have predicted and prevented the events of 11 September 2002.

Since Daniel Ellsberg's Pentagon Papers in 1971 and Peter Wright's autobiography *Spy Catcher* in the UK in 1985, governments have found it increasingly difficult to prevent secure information from being released. That challenge increased by an order of magnitude when the internet provided a global uncontrolled means of communication from the mid-1990s.

As democracies grow and progress they move through cycles of strong dominant leadership through to inclusive social policies and redistribution of wealth. Information transparency and its antithesis, propaganda, also have synonymous cycles. The interaction of different cycles compels them to balance their national interests with global events.

Through the culture of globalisation, information has gained greater freedom of movement. This has engendered a more 'bottom up' world, where information is profuse and no longer controlled by governments, who traditionally use a top-down approach to communications.

Figure 1.2 Spans of influence

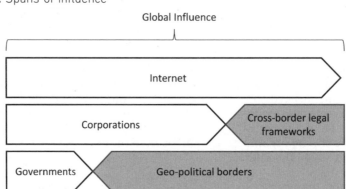

There are two answers to this conundrum. The first is that governments will need to organise their information using ECM principles. This means that tighter security can be maintained for specific classes of information, analysis can be tracked to differing levels of secure information without revealing those sources and interpretation exists between security layers. It is not impossible to keep information secure; it is just more expensive.

The second answer is for an internet idea like WikiLeaks: a collaborative environment. If the US government does not have the capacity to manage or analyse the information it has, it should consider asking for that analysis from the internet community. This approach has worked well in the scientific community and the SETI initiative, for example.

Analysis is only good if it proves to be based on accurate information and if its conclusions or predictions come to pass. Once contributors publish their machinations can be assessed for subsequent accuracy. Analysts will focus on particular segments of information and become recognised for their expertise.

Therefore there is an opportunity to outsource the analysis of information for use by governments around the world. Hence it is shared, openly contextualised and semantically transparent.

The facts about the past are relatively unexciting. What is more interesting and challenging is the provision of a trusted and measured mechanism to predict what happens and being able to change or influence the outcomes.

Transforming paper into electronic documents

Process architects should be careful not simply to replace the physical paper process by its electronic equivalent. This approach creates more work during the transformation stages from paper to the electronic medium and back again. The human natural mechanisms relied on during a paper process, such as sifting or speed reading, are not available in the electronic medium. It is important to incorporate new processes or applications to meet the needs of stakeholders. The solution is to re-engineer the process end to end.

MEASURING AND VALUING CONTENT

One of the challenges in ECM is assessing the asset value of information for a business plan. It is important to assess asset value throughout the lifecycle, and to provide mechanisms for measuring the overall asset level. The information lifecycle model provides a focus on the valuation of content in the ECM system.

Figure 1.3 Valuing content lifecycle

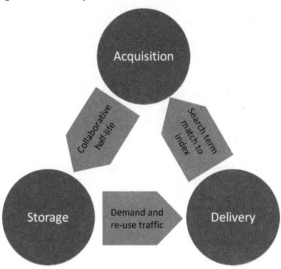

For the transition between acquisition and storage collaboration technologies provide a measure of half-life based on two things: the number of sustained content objects which are generated and the number of interactions for each object version.

Together these will give a time period during which a piece of content, on average across the organisation and all its content, is useful.

For the lifecycle between delivery and acquisition, the value of content can be assessed by determining the extent to which the attributes are complete for a particular content class. Historic reports of search terms captured during delivery allow analysis and an assessment of the indexing scheme's effectiveness. The indexing scheme can then be fine-tuned to improve delivery or reduce the burden and cost of categorisation.

For the simpler mechanism of delivery, statistics can be gathered to determine the number of times a content object is retrieved. They can include a measure of association with other objects to reveal relationships between content.

Organisations which understand the relationship between their content objects can start to determine which content objects bind, and attract stakeholders to, their repository. By doing so, they enhance the stickiness of their content overall. Key performance indicators (KPIs) should be created to enable a measure to be included in corporate reports.

SUMMARY

We have introduced the three core processes for ECM: acquisition, storage and delivery. Each can be defined by addressing the enterprise, content and management perspectives in which they operate. An organisation will need to define the solution in the nine areas to provide a cohesive and complete delivery model for ECM.

We have also introduced the concept of measuring content's value. Its incorporation is an important part of sustaining and measuring benefits, and of responding to changes in the markets in which the organisation operates.

2   ORGANISATIONS

There are unknown knowns:
the ones we don't know that we know
What US Defense Secretary Donald Rumsfeld didn't say on 12 Feb 2002

Organisations need to value what they inherently know. Yet, to cite a universal corporate truth, many still do not know what they know, something that the former US Defense Secretary neglected to admit.

There are a number of ECM concepts which organisations embrace to understand how they manage and work with information:

- **relevance:** why information is important;
- **retention**: what information needs to be kept;
- **timing and throughput**: when the information needs to be acted upon;
- **responsibility** and **contribution:** who manages the information effectively, and how they are motivated and rewarded;
- **ubiquity**: where the information can be accessed;
- **analysis** and **meaning**: how the information is interpreted, created and managed.

Their aim eventually is to know that what they know is valuable.

RELEVANCE AND RETENTION OF INFORMATION

Organisations are natural conduits for information. By their very existence they acquire and generate information through systems, processes and people.

In a simple organisation, where there is no automation in the capturing of transaction data and no system to transform paper into electronic form, the arbiters of information will be people. If defined at all processes will be centred on paper, and files as collections of paper. The capacity of the organisation to manage changes in demand for its services, or in its processes, will be severely reduced by its reliance on people to process information.

The organisation will need to make a judgment as to how relevant and valuable the information is when deciding whether to retain it. ECM as a discipline provides the means to manage retention based on whether the information is relevant to any of the enterprise core processes.

As an organisation develops and grows it starts to increase its channels of information management. It must communicate with more suppliers and work with more designs and products, all of which requires new information structures: electronic images, emails, photographs, CAD files, etc.

Good ECM practice ensures that the organisation catalogues all the mechanisms through which information is captured, managed and distributed. The catalogue can then record the use of such mechanisms and attribute costs to maintaining and transforming them, as well as valuing them.

TIMING AND THROUGHPUT OF INFORMATION

ECM recognises that the timing and throughput of information is an important factor in understanding when best to work with information. Some organisations have sparsely distributed systems and people, operating a policy of energy conservation. They react slowly to their environment but instinctively in tune with the business ecosystem in which they operate. Survival is the goal here, and information is maintained austerely.

Other organisations are highly active, producing a tremendous amount of information as they operate, busily reacting and growing. They are hives of activity, relying on the productivity and motivation of their people. Their survival is loaded with risk but their size enables them to keep going in spite of obstacles and failures. Most organisations however are a mix of these extremes.

ECM considers the need for collaboration and the management of processes. In doing so we catalogue the different paces and demands of each part of the organisation, from front office to back office. It co-ordinates, streamlines, reduces bottle-necks and allocates capacity where it is needed to retain a smooth information flow without the organisation seizing up.

For example the finance industry has traditionally managed its business in response to demands of front office staff to react at the pace of the market. At the same time its back office staff ensure that the business remains compliant, solvent and able to record the trades of its front office.

Executives and business leaders often perceive that their organisations are either swamped by information or unable to make effective decisions without all the information to hand. These are symptoms of an inability to recognise the differing throughputs required throughout the organisation, something that an ECM strategy addresses.

CONTRIBUTION AND RESPONSIBILITY FOR INFORMATION

Information technology has changed the demographics of business support. The secretaries and typing pools of the past are long gone: individuals now manage their own document generation and organisation. The internet has made information available at all times without the need to go to a library. Search engines have displaced librarians as the internet unites information from around the world.

As people in the organisation analyse information, they take the first step towards achieving knowledge by defining the rules, algorithms and limitations in which an organisation can operate. This knowledge can be represented by process maps, rules engines and content asset repositories.

The steadily managed and conceived knowledge must be accepted, referenced and adopted by as many people as possible to be sustained within the organisation.

As more information is generated the need to employ people to extract, mine and repurpose it in order to maintain the corporate knowledge grows. Knowledge workers are valued for their analysis of a specific area or subject matter expertise. Recent research has indicated that, although young people under 35 are able to gather information quickly, they do so superficially because they belong to the web generation. Their acquisition is highly tuned but their retention and ability to make comparisons are impaired. The new generation is likely to be more adaptable but will need support to retain and manage information with systems provided by organisations.

The principal proposition for universities is that they encourage people to learn continuously and engage in deep analysis to develop their ideas. The web generation has now embraced the universal idea of continuous learning but forgone the need for deep analysis. Analysis is stimulated by the opportunities in business or by global interest organisations (such as Wikipedia). Knowledge workers will use research skills to define problems and identify alternatives, solve them and try to influence corporate decisions, priorities and strategies.

The enduring success of the internet is its demographic and sheer size. Organisations must avoid adopting techniques which work well with the economies of internet scale but falter within smaller confines of a business. For example a search of a company website for a word may either reveal no results or many with equal ranking. The internet would statistically ensure that this wouldn't happen, yet for an organisation it is a perennial problem. This is resolved by adopting specialised roles to maintain and scrutinise information assets.

Mankind's knowledge has developed through the written word collated into books. Books become references of the current and accumulated knowledge of subject areas. They are signposts from which others can track their journeys.

To become a milestone a book or its electronic equivalent must:

- provide guidance on context and draw up a hypothesis or model of understanding;
- describe scenarios on past events and their effects within the model;
- suggest approaches and predict new goals and future challenges to perfect the model.

The book construction process works because for hundreds of years the editor's skills assured that contributions were clear, concise and conclusive before being published. For other media such as art, film, sculpture or audio or video, the signpost tests apply as well. Each medium develops a context and a means of producing stories which develop scenarios and actions. These can be developed as a snapshot represented by a photograph, a sequence represented by a film or indeed a business process map.

Snapshots exist as milestones in capturing knowledge. In the construction of documents which form the central components of ECM, these are known as records and represent a considered step in the improvement of knowledge. The challenge for many forms of knowledge is the final milestone test, to challenge the actions, assert methods or indeed to allow clarity of thought. The combination of all these forms creates the record. In ECM collaborative spaces the record constitutes all the documents and evidence which support the hypothesis or solution.

ECM defines the roles which an organisation needs to ensure that its knowledge remains consistent and current:

- Librarians ensure that information is up-to-date and correctly referenced.
- Designers scrutinise, index and determine whether information is relevant and represents an asset.
- Analysts improve and complete the information to determine trends.

Every organisation has the mission, ethics and culture by which it creates a product or service. ECM addresses the problems of the past by reducing the idiosyncrasies and inconsistencies manifest in the collation of different perspectives. It does so by ensuring that the right people are engaged in the right roles.

UBIQUITY OF INFORMATION

Organisational knowledge is that sustained by an organisation for its lifetime. However the essence of the organisation does not come purely from its directly employed staff, but all contributors, customers, stakeholders, market experts, pressure and common interest groups etc. Business networks, a combination of social media and collaborative tools, put greater value on knowing people who might know something beyond the need to share information.

To start sharing knowledge, trust must be built through personal networks. The free movement of labour and its involvement in initiatives is key to this. To do so expertise will need to be independent and have flexible hours, a situation that is becoming more common. Inevitably knowledge workers are less likely to belong to a large organisation than salaried staff, but will work in the same way as the film industry: freelance experts who collaborate just for the project.

The output of knowledge workers rarely sustains beyond the project. This adds to the difficulty of recognition and makes retention challenging. Just as filmmakers have their last project distributed for posterity, so knowledge workers require that the organisations they work for recognise and retain the results of their efforts. It is a waste to the organisation not to have a repository of information and knowledge. Therefore the goal for an organisation is to make its information ubiquitous and available beyond its natural boundaries: to become an enterprise which values its culture beyond its borders.

ECM provides good knowledge management, thus permitting an organisation to:

- sustain and recognise the contributions of all the stakeholders who add value to the organisation;
- provide guidance from a number of key perspectives for the organisation;
- supplement knowledge in the future and in different scenarios;
- make information universally available, and linguistically clear.

ANALYSIS AND MEANING OF INFORMATION

In scientific circles there is a general recognition that a great deal can be gained by having specialists in one discipline work in another. This means that the wisdom from one perspective in one science can sometimes provide groundbreaking methods for solving problems in others.

Cross-fertilisation is an important technique for breaking barriers to knowledge growth. It is a mechanism used in business intelligence technology which derives dimensions of information and compares and overlays different domains.

There is a correlation between data, information and knowledge in terms of quantity and quality (see Figure 2.1 Quality and quantity of content).

Figure 2.1 Quality and quantity of content

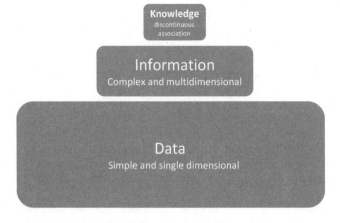

The quantity of data compared to information and knowledge is large. The reason data have low quality from a knowledge perspective it is that they rarely have context in terms of other data. To improve quality we combine data from multiple dimensions so that they have context and deeper meaning: the process of business intelligence and creating cross-references makes information more valuable.

ECM suppliers have begun to embrace the visual concepts of business intelligence to represent and transform the information in content so that it can be compared in more than one domain. An example is the crossing of sentiment to the implied object of the text to determine how people are feeling about topics which are important to them.

Business intelligence applied to content provides discontinuous association with the understanding that information can be applied to a completely different context or scenario and still be useful. Knowledge serves discontinuous association provided by cross-fertilisation or the juxtaposition of two disciplines. Each model of understanding should be universally understood and managed within the organisational body of knowledge. It must always be able to be added to rather than replaced.

Any knowledge system therefore must:

- be able to be accumulative and incremental;
- engage with all interested parties;
- be universal.

Two of the key challenges to compiling all-encompassing global co-operative knowledge are language and taxonomy.

Markets adopt taxonomies that describe their domains of expertise. The next step for organisations is to have forms of communication which are richer than the written word so that they can bridge language barriers. Candidates for these forms are videos, engineering diagrams, and sound. These in turn will give birth to new forms of taxonomy. The global span of the internet ensures that every subject under the sun can have an expert. The strange, extreme and esoteric can now persist. Social media tools are now available to ensure that anybody can find something or someone with whom to collaborate and find common purpose. The challenge is to bind the information from all these diverse perspectives without taking away the flexibility of the current simplistic information tools. Standards committees, under the umbrella of the World Wide Web Consortium, better known as W3C, are a source of progress in this area.

ECM recognises the importance of semantics throughout the internet. Under the guidance of W3C, the semantic web promises to break the barriers of language and open up taxonomies to address the complications of the world's social and business languages. It facilitates the creation and use of taxonomies to bond organisations or markets' participants. It can help to manage the accumulation of knowledge and collaboration for its improvement whilst permitting universal access: all the characteristics of a knowledge system.

SUMMARY

ECM practice catalogues the many mechanisms for information capture, management and distribution. It attributes cost and assesses the value of retention. It advocates collaborative processes to reduce process bottlenecks and capacity issues.

ECM strategy addresses the differing throughputs of the organisation to ensure that there is no information overload. It defines the roles which an organisation needs to ensure its knowledge and the information it is based on remain consistent and up-to-date.

ECM provides the goals for good knowledge management within an organisation to:

- sustain and recognise the contributions of all the stakeholders who add value to the organisation;
- provide guidance from a number of key perspectives;
- have information added in the future and in different scenarios;
- be universally available and linguistically clear and unambiguous.

In ECM collaborative spaces the record constitutes all the documents and evidence which support suppositions.

ECM recognises the importance of semantics in breaking language barriers to overcome the linguistic complications and colloquialisms of the world's diverse social and business languages.

ECM advocates and facilitates the creation and use of taxonomies to establish a common language and meaning throughout an organisation and the markets in which it operates.

3   CONTENT MATURITY MODEL

To exist is to change, to change is to mature,
to mature is to go on creating oneself endlessly
Henri Bergson

Transformation is not an overnight affair. For the organisation to achieve the improvements brought by an ECM approach, change needs to happen in stages: in deliberate steps within a programme.

Each step in accomplishing the ECM goals requires an assessment of where the organisation is. In line with business case planning there must be some means to measure improvements necessary to sustain the programme.

The ultimate goal is an organisation that is well governed. The assessment and guidance provided in this chapter aims to create an information management strategy. Each step needs to show corporate gains. Where the required investment is substantial these gains must be significantly larger.

Maturity models were originally developed in the mid-1980s. They were originally aimed at objectively assessing whether contractors have the capability to complete a project, by evaluating and improving their development processes. They have been used extensively throughout industry and government, applying to capability maturity in project management, maintenance, information technology and risk management.

The content maturity model has been derived from those original models but with a focus on ECM disciplines and content specifically within an organisation. It is a set of stages which encapsulate the behaviours, processes and systems in an organisation that can reliably produce effective outcomes.

Maturity models can be used by organisations in the same market to benchmark against the capability of their competitors. However this maturity model discussion specifically determines the starting point. It also considers others' experiences and provides a common language, a framework for prioritisation, and a means to define the measureable improvements. Many organisations do not know whether they are equipped to transform information into knowledge and enhance its overall value, especially with ECM as one of their tools.

We have established six core capabilities in the previous chapter that we will now use in the content maturity model:

- relevance – why information is important;
- retention – what information needs to be retained;

- timing and throughput – when the information needs to be acted upon;
- responsibility and contribution – who manages the information effectively and how they are motivated and rewarded;
- ubiquity – where the information can be accessed;
- analysis and meaning – how the information is interpreted, created and managed.

Against each of these capabilities, we focus on the dimensions which an organisation can change: people, processes and systems. Like many maturity models, the content maturity model shows how well an organisation is equipped to manage content and information through a number of competency stages.

THE FIVE STAGES OF THE CONTENT MATURITY MODEL

The five stages of the content maturity model are relevant across most organisations, no matter what their size is. It is important to recognise that it is based on competency rather than capacity: a single person or a large multinational will have different capacities for managing information. However they could both have the range of skills to manage it through to its ultimate business value.

The five stages may simply be represented by:

(a) individual;

(b) team;

(c) enterprise;

(d) optimise for acquisition;

(e) innovate for growth.

Each organisation will want to follow the trajectory from individual through to the ultimate proposition of innovation for growth, as each perspective improves on the last. The model or its framework determines what the organisation needs to do to move from each stage to the next.

The example above, Figure 3.1, is taken just after a business process re-engineering exercise. The organisation's people may be working as individuals and their process is defined to work across the organisation, but the systems are only deployed to service specialist groups.

The aims of the content maturity model are to

co-ordinate people, processes and systems to work from the same organisational perspective and;

to improve the organisational perspective towards innovation.

Figure 3.1 Content maturity model

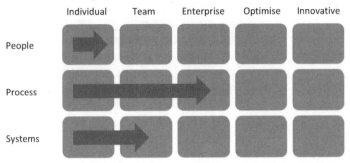

Most organisations today are positioned between stage 2, team, and 3, enterprise, simply because ECM tools and techniques are emerging in these organisations but struggling to make the single department solution universal.

It might be argued that innovation can happen before optimisation for acquisition. Organisations which are highly geared to research and innovation, for example pharmaceuticals and universities, are costly to run because their processes and systems have not been optimised. They also tend not to be voracious entities for external acquisition, but prefer internal organic innovation as a means to grow. They survive because society places a high value on health and education.

The content maturity model recognises the strengths and complexities across the dimensions at each stage, and that concentrating on one aspect alone is not an effective way of moving forward.

DIMENSIONS OF THE CONTENT MATURITY MODEL

For each of the three dimensions – systems, process and people – there will be different goals to reach each stage. First let us examine the three dimensions and what they mean.

People
There are many aspects to the people equation. These include not just the people themselves, but their support, skills, training, relationship to risk and reward and performance management.

There is also another aspect which is greater than the personal one: the organisational perspective or culture that the organisation brings. This can include social influences and collaborative environments which may or may not

Figure 3.2 People dimension

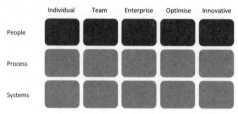

be linked to work. Informal hierarchies and email chains, all point to an organisation layered in many different ways.

People management considers certain characteristics that match the capabilities within the content maturity model. These are:

- timing and throughput – when the information needs to be acted upon;
- responsibility and contribution – who manages the information effectively;
- analysis and meaning – how the information is interpreted, created and managed.

All of these capabilities are influenced by the important people dimension.

Processes
The processes in this dimension are those of the business through which information passes.

Figure 3.3 Processes dimension

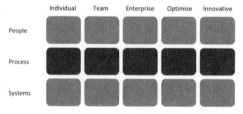

They take many forms: standards, guidelines, policies, record, information management policies and the workflow of everyday processes as information passes through the business.

Processes have certain defining characteristics which again match the capabilities within the content maturity model. They are:

- relevance – why information is important;
- retention – what information needs to be kept and when it is to be destroyed;
- timing and throughput – when the information needs to be acted upon;
- responsibility and contribution – who manages the information effectively.

Systems

Systems are the hardware, software and applications which create, store and manage information. The scope of systems and their technology is wide. They range from paper-based filing systems to a suite of fully automated electronic publishing systems.

Figure 3.4 Systems dimension

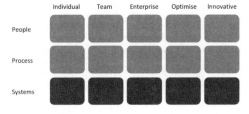

We would expect systems to have characteristics which can match the maturity model capabilities such as:

- retention – where information needs to be kept;
- timing and throughput – when and whether the information can be processed;
- responsibility and contribution – the security and tracking of managing information;
- ubiquity – enabling the information to be accessed from anywhere;
- analysis and meaning – helping the interpretation, creation and management of the information.

All of these capabilities are in some respect improved, managed and measured using ECM systems.

STAGES OF THE CONTENT MATURITY MODEL

Having described the dimensions and the characteristics by which each is measured, we shall now consider the five key stages of the content maturity model, and the dimensions in each stage and combination of dimension and stage. As we discuss each we need to consider the organisational perspective and determine whether it is relevant to the organisation. As the characteristics of the organisation are recognised, note the stage it has reached and determine what capability measures are appropriate for the specific dimension.

The Individual Stage

The individual stage is characterised by an individual's perspective. This individual is the owner of information who is in daily control of it and deals with the problems of maintaining it.

Figure 3.5 Individual stage

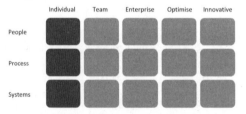

In small organisations, where personalities may be more important than teams, this is a default situation. It can be characterised by charismatic leadership that has ultimate authority over decisions based on information only it has.

Little power of thought and decision is down to the individual. However, in an autonomous way, individuals may be working for themselves with their own goals and rewards. Hence use of information is normally non-uniform. It may as a result seem subjective and vulnerable to criticism or interpretation, lack diligence or be inconsistent in detail. The individual will probably operate in his or her way and be likely to show the ropes to new employees in a paradoxically grudging but exuberant way.

The organisation therefore turns out to be a collection of self-interested personalities, which flourish at the expense of the organisation. With this in mind it is very difficult to get a consistent set of information about products and progress. Inevitably there is a distinct lack of organisational innovation. The market in which such an organisation works tends to be mature. On that basis there is a lot of wasted effort and slack capacity within the cash-cow of a single product or service.

Without the process for sharing information, success or failure, it is unlikely that the success borne out of a lot of hard work will be repeated. This is because the success is down to the individual, not the organisation. The future for the organisation is based mostly on luck and ruthless ambition: it is a compliance nightmare. If one sees maverick, non-conformist players and egos in this environment, there is a high risk of non-compliant processes which are difficult to audit, monitor and correct.

Individual – people
At the individual stage people will rarely work together or in teams. This would risk proving their incoherent methods to be flawed or open to question. The internal organisation will be fractured and unable to grow because the decisions of its in-house employees are ineffective and undeliverable. The content and information it holds consists of empty marketing slogans, which will mean little to the customer and result in few sales.

Change, although destabilising, is a lucky break for those individuals who thrive in the ensuing chaos. Egos and strong characters thrive whilst personal development is put on hold as a sacrifice to the rest of the organisation. There is no reward for promoting personnel by passing on lessons learnt, as no ECM environment is used to capture these.

Where dramatic change is in the air and information is inconsistent, the organisation's culture may be infused with erroneous rumour. The culture may also mean that fewer people work together in creating new products but simply join in for a quick gathering, before being thrown to various parts of the organisation without ever touching base again. Because of the lack of decision making based on good information governance, performance evaluation is usually weak and not followed through.

ECM capabilities will measure the extent of these behaviours by asking the following pertinent questions:

- Who helps us in making decisions and with what information?
- Who is responsible for the accuracy of the information and its completion on time, and for keeping records of the work done?
- Is the analysis open to verification, amendment or review? Do we have peers inside or outside the organisation who can influence our solution?
- Who is involved in correcting problems, and are the solutions recorded?
- How many people outside our immediate team or work environment understand what we do and contribute to improving the decisions made?

When these questions are answered, we know whether the organisation's people are entrenched in the individual stage.

Individual – processes

Processes can be defined poorly in unavailable documentation. This drives members of the organisation to adopt their own processes, which are often ad-hoc and unverified.

Acquisition of new information is carried out in a piecemeal and erratic manner using different timelines. Therefore it is inconsistent throughout the organisation as different people use it at different times. This gives rise to information gurus or power freaks who decide that they know more about the business than the business does because they have 'their' secret view that permits them insight into future trends. Again, if placed under scrutiny, these so-called mines of information turn out to be duplicates of outdated information. Often individuals' perspectives mean that, although they consider themselves blue-sky thinkers, their whole day is spent manipulating minutiae from which little can be gleaned statistically in terms of planning or strategic direction.

The process characteristic demands that the following capabilities are measured. In terms of the individual stage the following questions can reveal the weaknesses in the organisational process:

- How relevant is the process to the rest of the organisation?
- When is the source information or the result useful and how long can it remain so?
- Do we have all the information to hand to make a decision, and what happens when we have more work than we can cope with?
- Who is responsible for the accuracy of the information used? Who is responsible for the end-to-end process?

When these questions are answered we know whether the processes are bedded in the individual stage.

Individual – systems

At the lowest level this part of the content maturity model is formed around personal systems. These are paper files or electronic systems, which are rarely shared or networked on a consistent basis and do not refer to central information repositories. The original paper files may always be outside the filing system, with a place holder permanently in place.

There is very little scope for adopting collaboration tools or a governance approach on a common basis. Basic PC applications with plenty of specialised applications and spreadsheets tend to permeate this environment.

The costs of maintenance for security or safety through information duplication and access are large at this level. However the risks in terms of loss are low, because people have responsibility for their own work. The likelihood is that there is little governance. It is unlikely that the person has much access to, or control over, current content.

If we measure against the relevant capabilities we will see low scores for questions such as:

- What retention policy is there and who controls it?

- What capability is there to manage throughput on demand and change?

- What systems monitor responsibilities for the information?

- Which systems can be accessed, which systems have information and who cannot access the information?

- Are there systems to help interpret correct information and how do we know if it is correct?

- Do we have specialist skills and working tools which others may not understand?

Overall, from an organisational point of view, the systems perspective of the individual is anarchic and has a tenacious tendency to lack control.

The team stage

The team stage has been designed to represent ECM's natural organisational groups or teams working on projects. It is usually created in an ad-hoc manner rather than set in the divisional structures in which operational groups exist.

Figure 3.6 Team stage

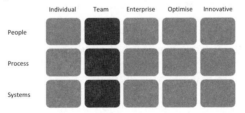

In ECM there is an organisational aptitude to consolidate information and bring together knowledge and people. Systems start to work at functional and departmental levels. Although silos of information still exist, at least all people in a particular division or department work with common information sources and start to share resources.

This results in significant effort to bring information across team boundaries so that it can be used consistently. There is therefore still a substantial cost linked to information management through the need to integrate its results manually. In the ECM world this results in re-keying data and content into different systems or having import/export or transformation tools to share data between groups.

In this model the dispersal of information and content results in inconsistent sources. Customers may see an instruction manual which does not reflect the product made by the production line. This usually happens with images of the same product being a different colour.

The deep entrenchment which happens from having departmental groups means that this interim stage towards building an enterprise may see little or no contribution between groups who are struggling to survive. There tends to be no co-operation contributing to the greater good of the organisation.

Team – people

People may be organised to manage projects at a departmental level. Team members are grouped together normally in static or cross-competency groups. ECM may be used to bring together virtually groups from dispersed regions and with different perspectives or interests defined within their organisation's social networks. This makes these groups functionally richer.

However there are still likely to be some cultural issues with teams working across departments because of differences in terminology or working practices. Now teams and tribes are defined there will be antipathy between groups who profess more competency and worth in contributing to profit.

Two questions need to be asked.

First, is the method of compensation clear, transparent and equal between departments?

Second, is the contribution from each department self-evident or is there a need to publicise the work of a specific ugly duckling department? If there is an ugly duckling department, why is it so?

Cultures which promote an inter-departmental competitive attitude to achieving performance improvements mean that information may become entrenched in silos and unavailable for sharing. This can be a result of having single skilled teams, usually following optimisation, in which information is only shared between those who have a common interest. The departments protect their information to ensure that their group is promoted above others. Managers use all their budgetary powers to ensure they have control of the information that they provide. This is so that they manage its value and can bask in the apparent success long enough to keep their jobs and annual bonuses. The solution to breaking this inter-competitive culture is to have multi-disciplinary teams or cross-enterprise governance teams which enable project and programme management.

The questions to ask are:

- When and if departments work together, do they accomplish work more quickly and effectively or do projects run into difficulty?

- Do projects cost more because some teams or departments drop the ball when taking responsibility for deliverables or benefits?

- Are there differences in the ways departments interpret information? Does information become difficult to merge because of its associative differences?

- Is it difficult to measure how the different departments contribute to the organisation? Are reward systems under strain because of high attrition rates?

- Are people frustrated by the loss of documents and information because the tagging or filing of information is incomplete?

When these questions are answered, we know whether the people in the organisation are working effectively in teams and across departments.

Team – processes

Through ECM, process management tools are starting to make an impact at this point. Workflow systems can manage the processes between applications but not teams. Processes are now likely to be consistent as people in the organisation start to recognise that sharing information and processes benefits their own process.

More project and planning tools start to be used because people start working as teams. Where there are teams ECM holds that there is a natural and effective opportunity for a project management office (PMO). This generates and maintains documents and information, and steers the organisation towards self-governance.

Based on the information provided by the PMO, project performance starts to be measured and compared, but not necessarily against KPIs at the enterprise level. For each KPI there are still multiple perspectives, which end up with differing outcomes:

- How relevant is the process to that defined by the PMO governance system?

- When is the source information adopted by the PMO or the result reported on, and how long before it becomes an action? How many layers of reporting are required to reveal the true status of all projects?

- Is information now worked through project boards which use a standard repository for all project documentation to make decisions? Is all the information on which decisions are made in the PMO governance repository?

- Is there a governance and responsibility matrix provided by the PMO? Does the organisation now have published and up-to-date organisation charts, with key stakeholders identified and kept informed of project issues through the central repository?

When these questions are answered, we know whether the processes are working across teams and departments.

Team – systems
The team environment covers shared information sources and common applications which add information to common resources depending on the department functions. Email systems still tend to be diversified because they still work along enterprise lines. However organisations sometimes have other communications channels that personnel prefer, such as minutes or SMS.

Customer data is probably not included in master data management principles. Some teams may use sophisticated tools that are not used across the whole enterprise. Conflict may start between departments who share data but interpret and use them differently.

Some of the qualifying questions that may be asked are:

- What information does the team create and who controls it?
- What capability is there to arbitrate throughput on demand and change with other teams?
- What systems pass on responsibilities for the information? Do we require customers to keep records of contracts? Do we use the email system as the system of record and exchange?
- Which systems are accessed and shared with other departments and who controls their development?
- Do the systems require a good deal of checking to ensure that all are in alignment?
- Is there a master system to which our part of the organisation works?
- Do our systems have capabilities that are used equally by other parts of the organisation?

When these questions are answered, we know whether the systems are still working departmentally and in the team stage.

The enterprise stage
When information is managed at an enterprise level, information is geared to meeting enterprise and organisational objectives and measuring effectiveness with KPIs.

Figure 3.7 Enterprise stage

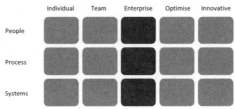

This means that departments, skills and competencies are joined end-to-end in fluid ways to satisfy the needs of the organisation and its customers.

There are probably still overlaps in capability between teams and departments as the enterprise has responded to the market and its customers. The organisation has increased its information flow and channels so that many more of its people have an information role. However at this stage there is little optimisation across the enterprise. The organisation will know what the value of its content and information is, as it determines where and what information is required to create value.

Processes start to become candidates for optimisation whilst being identified as core or non-core. Decisions become well informed through the use of ECM and enterprise-wide knowledge sharing. The cost of maintaining customer relationships goes down as products and services respond to markets with a clearer understanding.

There are still fundamental issues, such as whether the enterprise has the means to deliver, but the enterprise is now aware of the direction it needs to take. There is still plenty to do in terms of motivation and method, as well as transferring knowledge freely between departments.

Enterprise – people
In the enterprise-enabled organisation, people have a propensity to think beyond their own department. They can consider their overall effort and value to the enterprise or the organisation.

From a cultural perspective quality is paramount in an enterprise environment. In this way ECM reinforces the need to ensure that all documents, content and information are catalogued correctly, and that governance is paramount.

With ECM information is catalogued to become an asset. Without cataloguing it is worthless for leveraging value.

The questions to ask of the organisation people in an enterprise are:

- Do organisations, customers and partners accomplish work more effectively if they work together?
- Do projects cost more because the organisation or customer representatives fail to take responsibility for deliverables or benefits?
- Is there a difference in language between the customer and the organisation which produces disparities in services?
- Is it difficult to measure how financially healthy the organisation is in its market? Does it have trouble convincing the market of its plans and progress?
- Do loss of fidelity and contract proposition frustrate negotiation with partners?

Enterprise – processes

With clear and consistent processes now defined across the enterprise there is better governance of processes and change. There may be some capability to run analysis rather than simple reporting, although this is more likely in the next stage. The organisation works towards serving the customer rather than itself. Therefore relationship management features as a key product for its enterprise applications.

When customer relationships are managed ECM becomes more prevalent. It needs to draw on any number of communication channels, scanned documents, call records and so on to ensure a consistent record of interaction takes place for compliance reasons. In a true enterprise there is a thirst for governance and compliance: a subject for the next chapter.

There are now enterprise resource management systems to report on how well the whole organisation is working. Information becomes more transparent, predictable and consistent.

The questions to ask of the organisation's processes are:

- How relevant is the process to the interaction with customers and partners?
- When and how is the source information available to customers and partners to report on?
- Is information now worked through intranets and extranets which use a standard repository for all exchanges?
- Is there a governance and responsibility matrix provided by the PMO which includes customers and partners?

Enterprise – systems

Now information management systems are centralised with security and access well organised, all information growth is funded centrally and at an enterprise

level. Economies of scale become evident with elements of virtualisation to enable reuse.

A single version of the truth starts to permeate. At this point documentation is likely to be clearer and managed for change, with reporting systems consistently providing clear demographic reporting.

The following questions determine the extent to which the organisation has an enterprise perspective regarding its systems:

- What information is created by the enterprise and who controls it?
- What capability is there to arbitrate throughput on demand and change with customers?
- What other organisations pass on responsibilities for the information? Do we require partners to keep records of contracts? Do we use the email system as the system of record and exchange?
- Which systems are accessed and shared with other organisations and partners, and who is in control of their development?
- Are the systems self-optimised?
- Is there a market system to which the organisation works?
- Do systems have capabilities that are used equally by other parts of the organisation?

The optimise stage

This stage is the first under which an enterprise can adopt other business models and information sources readily from external parties. Once an organisation has this ability to optimise acquisition, it is ready to manage the final stage of natural innovation.

Figure 3.8 Optimise stage

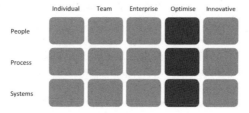

Acquisition means different things to different people. It can take the form of acquiring brands or growing the business by adding new capability.

A simple rule at this stage is that if we intend to innovate to stand still we are not truly innovating. Nor are we capable of growth, even organic growth. All facets of a business must be ready if it is to merge and acquire new businesses and information successfully. This then allows it to acquire innovative regimes and products which will sustain it in the future. Successful acquisition and incorporation of businesses drive us to build the mechanism to adopt and optimise new processes.

Other definitions might consider the organisation more adaptable and optimised whilst responding to changes. All these facets of behaviours are essential at this stage: adaptable whilst maintaining optimisation. If we rely on unverified and untrusted information then we may become slaves to it. Over-reliance on such information becomes a blind spot. Information governance, illustrated in the next chapter, guides an organisation in managing and sustaining trust in information and its sources.

Investment in partitioning and staging technology or platforms is required to bring external parties into the intranet or extranet whilst keeping our own organisation safe.

Optimise – people
What is most important in terms of people is the level of motivation which is evident as the organisation becomes more adaptable. A key tenet of compliance management is that all participants should understand the level of risk their role entails. Shared experiences from outside the organisation are exposed and the organisation encourages customer feedback and consultation.

Some questions to ask are:

- Are many people now information management analysts and self-starters?
- Is there a significant training programme to solve the issues of recruiting staff of the right calibre?
- Are people motivated by achievements and progression?
- Is there a free flow of interaction between people in different departments?

By this stage change becomes endemic but not stressful. The people are self-supporting on the past experience of achievements and market success.

Optimise – processes
The processes in the optimised and acquisitive organisation are tuned to maintaining power, speed and agility during choppy market conditions. Through ECM discipline the modelling of all processes has been achieved and

is available online for all people in the organisation to see and amend within a governance guideline.

Having a process feedback approach means that, when users enter a business process, they are rewarded with some information about the progress of their work package. This encourages them to participate and establish collaboration from the ground up.

With these measures the organisation tries to ensure that analysis can predict patterns of customer behaviour in spite of the changing market.

- Is there a process for continuous improvement?
- Do processes include partners and customers?
- Are there processes specifically for managing change?
- Are there core processes which are reused during the definition of new workflows?
- Are there metrics for market penetration in the marketing and sales process?

Optimise – systems
There are good migration strategies for any other products which may be acquired. The organisation has optimised its approach to adopting new businesses without overstretching itself. It has the capability to upgrade its systems seamlessly – or at least in a controlled way – and always considers being up-to-date with its technology key to remaining in step with the market.

At the acquisition stage decision processes and reports are particularly well honed. We would expect mergers or acquisitions to take no longer than three to six months, depending on the size of the organisation.

Organisations also have far reaching partnerships and intranets established so that they count their customers as part of their supplier chains. Customers are inextricably linked to the business: they do not just receive occasional emails about new products.

- Is there an architectural framework to configure the transformation and integration of technology?
- Are there levels of fault tolerance and data quality checks?
- Are there high levels of transparency in model documents where feedback and corrections are incorporated in the framework?
- Do all parts of the organisation have access to appropriate levels of information?
- Are business intelligence tools available?

The innovative stage

The principle behind the final stage is that the process for innovation is continuous and happens without the organisation stalling. Its components are all optimised and adapted to change.

Figure 3.9 Innovative stage

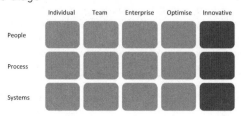

Innovation should not be considered a discontinuous process. Innovation is the prime approach for growth. Cash-cow products sustain longer because of their developed market penetration.

Being proactive is the best approach. An organisation should not have to wait for change to be thrust upon it, but should have the components and drive to make it happen. It is the ultimate goal for an organisation to define its market.

Innovative – people
At the innovative stage, all knowledge workers are largely proactive in their approach. They are able to react quickly to incoming issues but given time to manage creative thinking. The structure of the organisation is very loosely coupled, allowing scope for assembling everyone in interdisciplinary project teams at short notice.

People are engaged from concept to delivery, which makes for consistent and committed individuals. They engage in teaching and passing on their experiences at every opportunity. New ideas are captured and analysed. Intermittent associations are made with other industries and markets to achieve innovative leaps in products and services.

To verify the achievement of the innovative organisation for its people, ask the following questions:

- Is there freedom to expand beyond the boundaries of the business and explore new ideas without detriment to overall goals?

- Is there an expectation that people will act in entrepreneurial ways, but with consideration for balanced risk and investment?

- Has there been a good idea from a person not aligned with the focus of the business? Has this idea been adopted in the last six months?

- How diverse are the people? Do they span a variety of cultures and needs?

In the final melting pot experience is equal to intuition and creativity. Failure becomes a positive trait as the business manages it. This is like the instantiation of a project whose business case is changed: there is courage to take the lead but also to stop where the case no longer stands.

Innovative – processes

Processes in the innovative stage are completely represented in a flexible and universal process map which includes natural language rules and exception processing. All people in the organisation use the map on a regular basis whilst simulating and testing new process streams. Process interfaces work beyond the organisation's boundaries using arbitration web services. Process progress is also reported at various levels across the organisation using graphical means beyond the queue list.

Some testing questions about this stage would be:

- Is there a mechanism to keep updating older information by reassessment and re-innovation?

- Are there processes for capturing brainstormed ideas and collating them on a regular basis?

- Is there experience capture and is the process of learning made easier through organised knowledge and training systems, either online or using group gatherings?

- How long does it take for a new idea to come to fruition?

Innovative – systems

Systems of this nature are based on a likely set of bus-like infrastructure tools which provide a service-orientated environment. These are discussed later in the technical guide.

Infrastructure at this stage should be inherently flexible and extensible, with virtual, SaaS (Software as a Service) and multiple sourced environments for building and testing scenarios. The extensible nature of infrastructure should be enhanced through cloud technologies so that the cost of scalability and response is well controlled and financed.

The nature of the infrastructure is that it should support creativity through open communication, organised collaborative spaces, and manage policy and compliance complexity. It should foster clarity in business processes for everyone through ECM, from sources inside and outside the organisation.

- Does the organisation lead the way in products in its market?

- Has the organisation created new product lines?

- Has the organisation changed substantially and consistently over the past five years?

- Has the infrastructure responded and created better market penetration without loss of customer base?

- Is there a profusion of analytics tools?

SUMMARY

Using capability maturity models and the roadmap derived from them has been described as a long, hard and expensive experience, especially for large organisations. This is a fact of life for all large organisations which wish to optimise and change: their size causes natural inertia which prevents them from responding as a whole to events in the markets.

The way large organisations manage this inertia is by being geographically dispersed: having a global presence but with local perspectives. By doing so each branch responds without the possible burdensome controls that large organisations have to maintain. The majority of organisations are small to medium-sized, relatively autonomous and able to implement their strategies for change through the maturity model. This reduces the cost of doing so in an agile manner.

The content maturity model respects the three core components of an organisation: its people, processes and systems. It lays out a baseline for understanding across all parts of the business, simultaneously and in a co-ordinated manner. The next stage is to determine how to manage an organisation which has different levels of maturity for each component and how to align these. This detailed discussion will be left to the technical guide, which will describe how to manage and implement the roadmap.

From a technical perspective, following the assessment, the organisation will be ready to create an information management strategy and roadmap. These are also discussed in detail in the technical guide.

In the meantime if the ultimate goal of this ECM model is a well governed organisation, then we should look at that goal and see why it is important. We must understand that governance and compliance go hand in hand.

4   COMPLIANCE AND GOVERNANCE

Good government is no substitute for self-government
Mahatma Gandhi

We have seen what ECM can do in an organisation, and what approach to take when assessing the status of an organisation. We should now consider the organisation's goals, as a preliminary to developing the business case.

The fundamental goal in organisations and businesses is to be well governed. This is the measure of how well a company responds to direction from executives. To do so it should embrace both internal and externally driven compliance, and make that compliance good governance. As Gandhi implied, it is better to self-govern and regulate well than to have government thrust upon us, no matter how well intended that outside governance.

Governance is a self-compliance process: the adoption and recognition of best practice. It is policed by internal audit resources. Compliance is regarded as the application of external rules developed by industry safe practice through which organisations can manoeuvre. It is policed by external arbiters who represent the market or government. The ECM mechanisms used to manage both are the same. The opportunity is to use ECM to make both compliance and governance work.

CORPORATE GOVERNANCE

Corporate governance describes the laws, rules and customs governing the executive direction of an organisation. Governance can be democratic although is not necessarily. It should be fair, honest, transparent and representative of as many stakeholders' interests as possible, weighted by the political process through money, privilege or influence that wields power. A part of that process is a provision for recording decisions: this is a central tenet of ECM and supported by records management.

There are several dimensions to corporate governance, some quantitative and others qualitative. There are some working measures which respect democracy: promotion on competency, access to information, rights and responsibilities, and policies for privacy and legal obligations. Another set of dimensions is based on sustainability: social responsibility, economic employment activity, disability support and integration.

There is also a set of management measures in governance principally concerning executive accountability and competency for strategic steering and solutions. Other dimensions involve organisational structures and processes, strategic planning, resource efficiency, partner co-operation and training.

Information governance

Information governance is the cornerstone of governance and compliance. We have already seen one of the processes of information governance in our discussion: the cataloguing of information and its use throughout the organisation. Information governance aims to maintain standards, keep references and record corporate responsibilities to do with corporate compliance.

Information strategies, the subject of a technical chapter, have information governance as a key deliverable. Without it, information management business cases lose traction and potential benefits derail.

COMPLIANCE

Compliance is the act of adhering, and demonstrating adherence to, rules, standards, laws and regulations. These rules may be defined at different levels, from filling in timesheets punctually to working with global standards such as Sarbanes Oxley, Solvency II or Basel II.

There are several areas to consider when considering compliance:

- **Corporate** – the rules according to which an organisation works internally. These are normally aligned to best practice, securely maintaining intellectual property, financial authority, probity and liability. It is corporate compliance that is closely aligned with, and measures, governance.

- **Legal** – the rules within which legislative and market frameworks oblige an organisation to work. These are generally aimed at solvency, transparency, privacy and retention of proof of trading.

- **Contractual** - the rules according to which an organisation works with another. These cover obligations and responsibilities, and maintaining secure communications, confidentiality and records during the partnership.

Each industry has a specific set of rules in each of the above areas, with some rules running across all organisations and industries. The juxtaposition of rules and regulations in each industry, together with the level of change, make the process of understanding and adhering to those rules complex and difficult.

The challenge in compliance

All organisations should have a repository where critical business documents and information are stored. All personnel who have access to this repository will need to understand and apply the appropriate regulation for storage over a prescribed time. This requires training for personnel responsible for ensuring that copies are destroyed as necessary, that information can be readily retrieved, that it is catalogued to enable search and discovery, and that it is maintained as a single source of the truth.

The challenge to this status quo is that the number of systems generating data, and the respective data, increase exponentially on a daily basis. This makes it increasingly difficult to maintain a single repository which can scale and maintain compliance performance in submission, retrieval and discovery.

Understanding the regulators' perspective
Each of the institutions which formulate regulations and laws do so as parties with interests in protecting the market they represent or manage:

- The legal institutions do so to make the process of prosecution or defence as clearcut as possible. They aim to remove misinterpretation and misuse.

- Government departments do so to protect their citizens from foreign powers. For example they protect technical information for military application.

- Trade bodies do so to protect their markets from fraud or malpractice, to ensure a level playing field for all, and to ensure growth in the market and its subscribed participants. They allow participating organisations flexibility in operating at a profit by prescribing free market or liberal practices.

However we should be aware that some regulations can be ill conceived, ambiguous, outdated, too general or superfluous. Enforcing these can often depend on political expediency when socioeconomic circumstances change.

Most compliance standards, however, are sound and exist for good reasons. Issues only come about because they conflict with each other or affect the organisation by requiring layers of extra process.

Dealing with regulatory change
There are changes in all three categories of compliance, albeit at different frequencies. There are also changes to the technical infrastructure due to upgrades, reconfiguration and optimisation. Therefore technical solutions for compliance need to adapt to these changes, but also to be immune to the changes inherent in the management of IT systems.

In itself compliance is not just about understanding and managing logical integrity, but also managing physical integrity. As the compliance solutions are all pervasive, any organisational, operational or technical change will prompt a reassessment of the compliance solution. Let us consider a model that represents the components of compliance.

The compliance model, as shown in Figure 4.1, represents the markets and region and country boundaries, which often overlap. Regulations and laws apply in both these areas and organisations work through regulations to access

Figure 4.1 Compliance domains

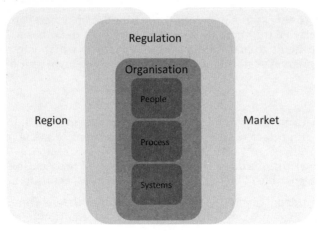

different markets and countries. Organisations contain components and resources which are affected by, and drive, compliance: people, processes and systems.

Markets

Market compliance typically originates in response rather than forethought. High-profile events stimulate governments to reassure citizens. For example the events of 11 September 2001 drove governments to introduce more stringent security regulations in the airline industry.

Market compliance evolved as a result of free-market policies in the latter part of the twentieth century. The deregulation of industries and markets was encouraged to free up trade and encourage competition. This *laissez-faire* philosophy, given the events of 2008 and the credit crisis, has consistently been under pressure to swing back towards a more regulated environment to ensure clearer financial risk management.

New or amended regulations are therefore typical when circumstances demand them. Where the organisation exploits weaknesses in market processes, in order to optimise throughput or cost of transaction, it will be open to interference in its key operational mechanisms.

Usually the presence of numerous and vociferous trade bodies and industry interest groups indicates the level to which regulation and standards need to be enforced. By trying to achieve self-regulation these groups try to avoid having legislation forced upon them.

Country- or region-specific

Regulations may be specific to a country or region because of the political will and energy of a government wishing to show that it can be strong in enforcing its laws, and independent of global practices. Depending on the stability of a country's political system, these regulations may be open to change.

An organisation may actually have unique and ring-fenced business models operating in particularly challenging countries to protect its core operations from the burden of change. Moving goods between countries is usually one of the largest challenges in managing a business, next to managing the free flow of labour.

An organisation needs to monitor political changes in the countries and regions in which it operates, to assess the risk of change and the impact of new regulations.

Regulation

Regulation is a constantly moving target which has to deal with constant innovation of regulated products.

ECM introduced the concept of e-discovery as the basis for retrieving information required by auditors or legal teams during investigations. It aimed to reduce the burden from regular audit and legal activity. It must be tempered by an assessment of the likelihood and frequency of such events.

Governments or market bodies respond to the need to audit and regulate. The cost of doing so can be high depending on the socio-economic circumstances. Regulators normalise economic intensity, offer guidance during recessions to encourage market activity, and increase corrective actions when markets are buoyant.

Basel II will affect IT compliance, as enough capital needs to be in place to cover potential risks. Systems that assess risk must report the right data with integrity and securely.

The UK's Data Protection Act, the Gramm-Leach-Bliley Act and other privacy laws compel organisations and their business partners to use information responsibly. Through information governance, ECM cataloguing and analysis have clarified the contractual arrangement for partnerships. They may entice organisations to give independence to highly distributed companies, in order to protect the organisation as a whole.

Outsourcing systems or data to a supplier does not absolve the organisation from the actions of that supplier. Partnerships are put at risk because of the information exchange protocols for controlling the transfer of personal information between organisations. ECM can provide audit controls for the exchange of data which conform to process rules, and controls which match policy and regulation guidelines.

Over $6 billion was spent on Sarbanes Oxley compliance in 2007, much of it wasted because businesses were only encouraged to focus on their key systems and processes. The cataloguing process within ECM enables organisations to understand what makes up their end-to-end, mission-critical and regulatory processes.

Organisations which try to stop some channels of communication drive their people to work through other, more accessible but non-secure methods. In this case ECM provides an auditable control of information passing through a channel, so that the traffic level and information passing through it can be assessed for appropriate security controls.

People

It is important that the people responsible for regulation manage the adherence to these rules and ensure that they are followed appropriately and consistently. People are inherently inconsistent in the way they interpret rules and act upon them. Managing people implies a constant need to train and refresh their understanding of the organisation's processes, and compliance implications. The key message should be that individual members of staff are responsible for the compliance of their tasks and that all relevant information is retained as evidence. As people are more changeable it is often better to automate practices through processes and systems rather than rely on people's goodwill.

Processes

A well organised business will define its processes so that all relevant personnel work consistently. Hence they can derive advantages from working to a common goal with an accumulative positive impact. Those in the organisation who don't work to these processes can produce a negative impact on the business.

A business which responds to market conditions and innovates to meet demand has to review and change its processes and business practices on a regular basis. These changes affect its compliance solutions.

New management, rather than acquisitions or mergers, carries the highest risk for compliance. New managers tend to create an impact by optimising systems and people under their control, with inevitable consequences for the compliance group. Being self-driven and self-budgeted operators, these managers rarely co-ordinate with compliance until it is too late. Audit then finds unreported and unapproved changes. Acquisitions and mergers tend to be strategically controlled from a higher level, and so to have direct and early involvement from compliance.

Consultants providing advisory services and facilitation for change and optimisation also affect compliance. The risk is relatively low, as good professional consultants should know to involve compliance in their work during the early management of stakeholders.

Systems

The introduction of any new technology into the business entails new security risks and hence increases exposure to regulatory issues. The increasing number of devices and channels of communication used in business increases security vulnerabilities. Fines have been imposed or levied on companies with an inappropriate management of information and content. Hence there is a need to have a securely archived communication channel, accessible through search facilities and monitored for use, security and integrity.

The mantra by which enterprise compliance solutions for ECM should be constructed is 'pervasive, not invasive'.

RECORDS MANAGEMENT

There is now an irreversible dependency on digital information. In spite of the business and social opportunities provided by such an accessible and available tool, it can be open to misuse and abuse. To counter the threat of legislation, standards and guidelines have been created to protect information.

The basic principle behind compliance through record management is that records are collections of interrelated electronic or physical objects or documents at a given point in time, rather than a single object or document. The main standards in Europe are through MoReq2, while in North America the Department of Defence Directive 5015.2 has created the similarly named standard.

In the ECM information lifecycle, described in detail later, a document may be the key trigger for a business process, such as an invoice for approval. Once approved and paid, this becomes less valuable and entails costs for the organisation, which has to store it for a legal corporate retention time of several years. This is where records management takes over.

To accept the process of records management requires the governance of documents through categorisation across the organisation. This is done through what is called the file plan – something which is challenging for organisations to define and maintain. The ECM cataloguing and information assessment creates the file plan as a matter of course.

Many understand the need to manage business processes through ECM as they add value in the day-to-day operation. But the process for managing records is ultimately a 'back-office' function that any organisation regards as adding to the bottom line.

There are technical challenges to having a good records management structure, because it requires access to the plethora of documents which make up the record. This access must have overarching control across a number of repositories to be effective. An ECM strategy which does not extend to managing records is therefore a short lived one, because ECM provides the technical means to bring these repositories together at the infrastructure level, rather than as an add-on through records management.

Basic statutory demands

There are three key statutory demands for this type of records management:

- corporate legal compliance for declaration of corporate records;
- freedom of information laws requiring a public authority to make its information open, through an information asset register providing guidance and policies on what information retained by the organisation should be made available and in what form;
- the Data Protection Act for personal information held by organisations – the process by which freedom of information is tested.

Very simple questions can be asked as we enter the records management realm: 'What documents are there? Where are they? And when must they be destroyed?'

One further process also needs to be defined in the ECM business: the declaration of the record. Further technical processes should be managed in the background: retention, destruction and auditing.

The following are also key business requirements:

- to be able to declare a document as a record or part of a record, within a representative collection or structure such as a hierarchy;
- to provide further attributes of that record (i.e. when it was declared and what its retention period is);
- to manage the disposition or destruction of records, usually through a retention classification process. Hence records acquire generic retention attributes or indeed instigate a 'legal hold' where all destruction for a class of records is suspended during an investigation or e-discovery;
- to manage the accessibility and security of records in the long term by assuring ECM security controls on the prevention of changes, for example through version control;
- to retain an audit trail of all ECM activities as a matter of course.

Records retention

In terms of solutions a business would expect:

- layered retention rules for ECM;
- automated retention and destruction;
- pre-defined classes of retention and attributes;
- automated declaration of business process.

An organisation must balance its need to keep information which is useful to its operation – usually enough to maintain annual reports and for over 24 months – with its need to maintain information for legal and regulatory purposes (seven years in the UK for example). Given the burden and concomitant costs of information management, the ideal is naturally to retain information for the shortest possible time.

Let us imagine the example of a manufacturer and its retention period for each class of information.

Table 4.1 shows how each department works within different timeframes for information usage. The purchasing department might work in one-month periods, operations might work in two-month periods, sales in quarters, finance in 12-month periods and support departments in three-year periods. The organisation may even have an historic archival process which retains records of historic or innovative significance as well as samples for viewing.

Table 4.1

Content and record	Period of retention
Product development plans and service support	3–5 years
Product manufacturing records (for fault adjustment where product takes 1 week through production)	1 month
Product sale records (for commission calculation)	3–6 months
Supplier invoices for materials and supplies	1–3 months
Product guarantee records	12–36 months
Product user manual	1–10 years
Corporate reporting	12–24 months

Typically each will have a different understanding of retention. There is therefore a need for a schedule or catalogue of all the record needs for each part of the organisation. It helps in:

- control and standardisation;
- rapid access and retrieval;
- enhancing and clarifying decision making;
- illustrating dependency in business process through asset association;

- fostering a culture of corporate compliance and accountability;
- streamlining process and reducing redundancy and optimising business processes.

There is a variety of retention periods depending on the industry or country. Examples are:

- medical records which have to be kept for the life of the person;
- insurance records which are normally limited to the period, but some insurance records need to be retained for 75 years;
- financial records which in some jurisdictions need to be in place for seven years;
- some countries require 27 years' retention for all personal records.

Further reading of MoReq2 and ISO 15489 is essential to understanding the scope of records management.

SUMMARY

We have established the ECM link between governance and compliance. We have illustrated that compliance can influence people, processes and systems, and be driven from a market or country-specific environments. Finally we have described the natural inclusion in ECM of records management to manage compliance processes, rules and retention.

5   DEVELOPING A BUSINESS CASE

There are risks and costs to a program of action. But they are far less than the long-range risks and costs of comfortable inaction
John F. Kennedy

Like any other business case the ECM case is a structured document. It provides a justification for investing in an ECM project or programme based on estimated costs, risks and benefits on completion.

It is imperative that a business case is established at the beginning of an ECM project. This allows executives and stakeholders to decide on the balance and priority of investment beforehand, reassess the project at suitable milestones and confirm the outcomes from the measured benefits at the end.

In line with respected project management practices such as PRINCE2, the justification should be continually checked to determine if it remains viable. If not the project should be suspended or closed down to take stock of any changes.

Executives need to remember that a project is a means to an end. If one project is stopped because of reduced justification, lessons will be learnt which can be taken forward to the next with a stronger case. This will make the latter project more likely to succeed.

The business case must be drawn up by the senior stakeholder, the person accountable for achieving the benefits. It should be underwritten financially by a senior executive, on the basis that the project offers value for money, is aligned to strategic objectives and can be delivered.

The scope of the business case will determine where benefits are realised. ECM projects are considered infrastructural in scope. Incorporating ECM technology typically requires the same disciplines as when a new fundamental infrastructural layer, such as security, network or virtualisation, is adopted. From an enterprise perspective the new layer needs to be available at all points in the organisation, as well as ready to integrate in all the major information systems. Refer to the Technical Guide: Architecture for more information on the technical approach to adoption.

STRUCTURE OF THE BUSINESS CASE

The subject areas of a business case are typically:

(i)   an executive summary;

(ii)   reasons ECM is needed;

(iii) business options, including doing nothing, so that each option has a baseline on which investment benefit can be measured for viability and value;

(iv) expected tangible benefits for each business option, in measureable and quantifiable terms which align with organisational objectives and information strategy;

(v) expected challenges to the consequence of actions on stakeholders;

(vi) timescales for the project and for benefits to accrue;

(vii) costs, including operational maintenance and finance of funding – regarded as the basis for investment appraisal;

(viii) risks which may reduce or enhance the benefits, or reduce or increase the cost.

It is worth describing in greater detail four items in this structure which play important parts in the business case:

(i) reasons for adopting ECM;

(ii) options for managing change;

(iii) tangible and intangible ECM benefits;

(iv) developing a roadmap.

Finally, and more important, we review the achievement of ECM benefits.

First the reasons for adopting ECM must be verified as requirements, and the ECM benefits realistically established. Then the various options which meet the requirements and provide clear sets of benefits need to be compared for cost and investment. This is the basis for the final choice, which will be the overall solution for delivery, as shown in Figure 5.1.

REASONS FOR ADOPTING ECM

There are key reasons a business might require ECM. In the discussion of the organisational aspects of information, there are six categories in which we can place the issues:

* relevance – why information is important;

* retention – what information needs to be kept;

* timing and throughput – when the information needs to be acted upon;

* responsibility and contribution – who manages the information effectively, and how they are motivated and rewarded;

* ubiquity – where the information can be accessed;

Figure 5.1 Emergence of the business case

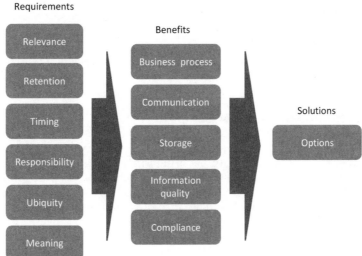

- analysis and meaning – how the information is interpreted, created and managed.

To summarise these in respect of a business case, there are some relevant questions for each. These can be asked during the assessment stage and maturity tests, before the business case is drawn up:

- Is the information valuable or relevant to its operational needs?
- Is the storage of paper taking up costly office space?
- Have key documents been lost within the organisation, either by mistake or malicious behaviour?
- Are personal email spaces limited and do they often exceed capacity?
- Does it take time for information to be distributed and processed?
- When dealing with customer records, are some files identified as lost or difficult to share across systems?
- Is the organisation reliant on what its people intrinsically know?
- Is information only available to those who need it if they know where to find it?
- Are there multiple systems being used to access the customer or operational records? Do these contain diverse and contentious information?

Many of these facets are intangibles of the business benefits analysis. Hence they need valuing and transforming into tangible measurable costs.

OPTIONS FOR MANAGING CHANGE

It is important that the options for adopting ECM technologies are clearly thought out through scenarios for managing change. A good option for one business is not necessarily a good option for another. The content maturity model, discussed earlier, provides some key milestones. However this will need to be supported by a roadmap or schedule so that improvements are co-ordinated.

TANGIBLE AND INTANGIBLE ECM BENEFITS

All improvement projects in an organisation have a mix of tangible and intangible benefits: those that can be valued in a straightforward manner – using monetary value – and those that cannot. The key to developing a successful business case is to ensure that tangible benefits are promoted and calculated wherever possible, because only the tangible benefits can be correctly valued and assessed by the financial officers.

The financial officers measure the benefits against the costs and assess whether the project should go ahead. To be successful in preparing a business case, avoid references to intangible benefits wherever possible. No business case will succeed if it is based on emotion and 'gut feeling'. All business executives and managers need to determine early on what the return and risk are.

DEVELOPING A ROAD MAP

Every business case must have a defined roadmap in which adoption of the benefits and the work undertaken is related to longer-term strategic aims. In developing a roadmap it is important to understand the two types of driver: business and technical. The roadmap records the drivers appropriate for the business at a specific time.

Typical business drivers are:

- the need for compliance from industry regulator both from an audit perspective and a reporting perspective;
- the need for optimised business processes, especially for client refocusing initiatives;
- the need for competitive advantage once processes are exposed and shared with the outside world;
- the need for cost reduction across the global operation without compromising quality or response of the customer;
- the need to achieve better product margins;

- the need to overcome operation reluctance to adopting process tools where there is a perception that they represent over-control and extra irrelevant tasks.

Typical technical drivers are:

- the need to upgrade components in a synchronised manner to avoid obsolescence;
- the need to improve performance bottlenecks induced by emergent implementation;
- the need to improve flexibility and definition of process management tools;
- the need to provide documents over the web for sharing globally;
- the need to provide collaboration over the internet to improve email and document synchronisation;
- the need to consider the value option for the best configuration of the document repository;
- the need to integrate with many different technologies in the process engine;
- the need to have a common component framework on which business applications can be developed.

As the roadmap emerges it will also track risks and benefits, so that it forms the core strategic plan for the business case.

REALISING ECM BENEFITS

ECM vendors are keen to provide a list of generic benefits, all or any of which may not be achievable and justifiable in the particular organisation. Therefore it is important that each benefit is carefully assessed within the context of the business as it stands.

We can take five candidate generic ECM benefits and see that they must be carefully considered in order to be effective:

- business process improvement;
- better communication;
- physical storage;
- information quality;
- compliance.

Business process improvement

More often than not it's not what employees know which matters. What is more important is how they work with the systems and regulatory environment.

Many organisations use people, like oil, to fill the integration gaps which exist between systems, knowing that they provide flexibility in managing or overcoming bad processes and information. An over-reliance on such resources increases the risk of information leakage.

Business process improvement, through business process management (BPM), is by no means a straightforward benefit to achieve. It requires effort to assess current practices, re-engineer them and build technology solutions which can effectively replace, supplement or enhance the work done by people.

An assessment of **all** current business processes and the options for their re-engineering should always be a precursor to adopting wholesale business process management. BPM is an infrastructural technology which is best adopted across the whole enterprise. Plans should always be drawn up to deliver BPM at all levels through analysis and agreement, before any technology is put in place. Always try to adopt process management tools with as diverse a set of requirements as possible, with both high and low levels of detail and varying levels of complexity.

It is good practice to prototype the technology in the context of the business and prioritise transformation projects to test its reach and effectiveness. Where personnel need to access several systems to get all the information at hand, ECM technologies are likely to help by bringing this information under one repository. ECM addresses document processes which are inefficient and slow in as they pass through too many hands, any more than three touches is too much.

ECM also understands when information is archaic – i.e. has not been rewritten or reviewed in the last five years. Where this is the case its value will be significantly lower from an accuracy and compliance decision perspective.

Where processes are not documented, or centrally accessed by all personnel, they are not measurable, owned or transparent. As the processes are not measurable they cannot be improved. As they are not owned, no-one is in place to consider, advocate and act upon improvements.

When there is a good deal of complexity in business processes, efficiencies always result when the processes become simpler. The cost of retaining business, as well as following up on new opportunities, can be linked to inefficiencies in capturing information and ingesting new market competitive information.

It can become increasingly difficult to get all the information in one view to support all key strategic decisions. This needs to be monitored over a period of time as the organisation deals with change.

Better communication

We live in an information society where we are encouraged to communicate and engage. It is inevitable that anything between 20 and 40 per cent of our time will be used to manage communication in various forms. We have faxes, books, emails, manuals, brochures, reports, spreadsheets, web pages, video and images. Some tools will be superseded by others, others will be sustained.

There are limits to the number of channels a person can communicate through. There are probably three to four different means of communication which a person will acquire or focus on. Personnel increase, on average, their use of all technology communication channels by 800 per cent over a five-year period. By 2012 it is likely that there will be 600 million more internet users than in 2009, with mobile use growing by 300 per cent and data overtaking voice in the mobile network.

As the microprocessor became pervasive in the 80s and 90s, wireless communication will become endemic. There will be an insatiable need for receiving and generating information from new devices such as satellite navigation, metering systems and radio frequency identification devices (RFID).

Businesses today have adopted email as the appropriate means of communication across the enterprise. To date there is nothing more versatile and effective.

It is unlikely that ECM will bring better communication *per se*. One of the recurring challenges in ECM is the management of security and offline access to email when there is a transfer of access to a central repository from an email server. Incomplete technology implementations for security have resulted in emails to recipients outside the organisation having attachments to document repositories which are only accessible to those within it. This is particularly frustrating for the recipient.

In an increasingly disconnected and mobile computing world, people use technology which stores the attachment or documents on the mobile device. Hence it can be read offline and when the device is disconnected from the mobile communications network. Simple email readers may not have the capability to pick up these documents or work with them.

It is important to ensure that such technical idiosyncrasies are resolved early on. This is achieved by prototyping and formulating a security policy which encompasses all stakeholders, including customers.

Physical storage

Even when business activity abates during a recession, digital information created and transmitted still increases. Currently the 'digital universe', a term which encompasses all information that exists, is doubling in size every 18 months. This is far more exponential than the rate of increase in the scale and complexity of microprocessors, as expressed in Moore's Law.

The growth of email continues unabated. As more of the world's people become connected through mobile phones to engage in various means of communication – voice (with IVR) email, SMS and MMS – they tend to communicate on a number of different channels with increasing levels of traffic.

As emails proliferate so does the need to store and access them. Storing information costs money. During the ECM assessment process an analysis of whether the customer can be responsible for storing information is made. Other philosophies of information try to reduce information flow through the organisation.

Physical storage systems for paper need managing, and are inefficient because they require time to traverse and maintain. There may also be many unnecessary duplicates of paper documents or, indeed, unnecessary paper versions of electronic documents.

The cost of copying and maintaining printer supplies can be excessive, depending on the number of paper documents stored. There is likely to be an advantage in making a study of the trail of paper throughout the organisation in its lifecycle: where it is created, how it exits and to whom it goes. For electronic systems, reuse of expensive hard disk space is an issue if the purging or moving of the content to an archive is not under ECM control.

Considerable resources are often squandered in migrating to new technology platforms. The migration or renewal of major system components, which occurs more than once every three to five years, should lead to a reassessment of the stability of the technology choices.

The saving on physical storage of paper is often offset by the cost of maintaining technology to retain the electronic image. The cost of physical storage – whether off-site or on-site – needs to be consistently balanced with the ongoing costs of technology – on-site, managed off-site or outsourced – either of which can fluctuate as market demand and commoditisation dictates. The cost of increasing storage capacity is dependent on how well the enterprise can leverage economies of scale.

The advent of the computing age has not delivered the promise of the paperless office. Offices still need photocopiers and printers. But these devices are now multifunctional scanners, printers and copiers.

There is still a specific advantage if it can be measured: the cost of distribution and control. If the business has to move the paper around to all its offices, there are specific cost benefits to using electronic communication to transfer those documents but also to control their distribution so that master versions are always retained.

One factor which can help organisations manage the cost of their ECM implementation is the cost of storage. This should always be transparently allocated to the information owner and paid for by that part of the business.

The cost of the application and infrastructure must be paid for by central resources. However the cost of information storage must always be a direct contribution budgeted from the part of the business which uses it. If that part does not engage in optimising its information use, i.e. working better with emails, then it has to bear the cost. A centrally funded storage for records management should be retained, however: this encourages the organisation to be a part of the ECM process.

Information quality

The information retrieved may be proven to be incorrect. By implication the source, known or unknown, is shown to be untrustworthy. Where the source has authority it also has an audit trail based on solid, retrievable evidence which can be transparently made available for inspection.

Documents or emails may become misfiled in shared repositories, with confidential emails to one client being viewable with other clients' records without being redacted. The set of attributes for a particular document may be different, depending on which part of the organisation generated it. This makes it increasingly difficult for the organisation to share and find information, or to consolidate its view. Information is regarded as an asset, but the organisation doesn't seem to manage it like one. It doesn't know what information it has and where, making it difficult to value and maintain. Sometimes the organisation has the impression that it has little control on information. Information leaks at inappropriate times, or requires effort to be maintained or used consistently, and therefore to be of value. Personnel may not contribute their knowledge through sustainable documents into the organisation's systems. Personnel may spend more than 10 per cent of their time getting hold of authoritative information. Where this happens an assessment of the information required needs to be undertaken.

There may be too much information on which to make a decision, with the information not in a usable form. The information available may not be up-to-date, for instance. No record of its review, or the criteria under which it was accepted or agreed, may be available.

There is a fine balance in retaining enough information that the organisation remains operationally effective, consistent and solvent. Information is sometimes retained by personnel, as there is still a belief amongst the powerless that information is power. Over time this knowledge becomes anodyne as more information comes to hand. Teams of people sharing knowledge acquire and retain it better, although behaviourists may criticise those who repress independent thought for the profit of collective experience.

Compliance

Governments demand more transparency during collaboration, stringent controls on change and sourcing, and clearer responsibility for maintaining information. Regulators often require that businesses manage information using tools prescribed through ECM, so that information can be controlled and managed in a structured manner. As regulations and systems to enforce them become more effective, data deemed to be 'security sensitive' will increase by 50 per cent.

SUMMARY

We have reviewed the structure of the business case and reviewed the reasons for adopting ECM from the earlier chapters and considered those reasons against the set of benefits.

- relevance – why information is important;
- retention – what information needs to be kept;
- timing and throughput – when information needs to be acted upon;
- responsibility and contribution – who manages the information effectively, and how they are motivated and rewarded;
- ubiquity – where the information can be accessed;
- analysis and meaning – how the information is interpreted, created and managed.

We have been able to review and discuss the most important parts of the business case benefits and understand which are pertinent to ECM:

- business process improvement;
- better communication;
- physical storage;
- information quality;
- compliance.

This completes the business guide.

We have covered the introduction to ECM and its lifecycle. We have reviewed how the business uses content, information and knowledge, and its current capability through a content maturity model. We have addressed and reviewed any compliance requirements and brought all this together into a coherent, realistic and comprehensively covered business case.

PART 2: ECM TECHNICAL GUIDE

Evidence and reason: my heroes and my guides
Naomi Weisstein

This technical guide details the analysis, delivery and architectural scope for ECM. It describes how to:

(i)   manage and deliver change in the organisation and culture;

(ii)   progress through the content maturity model;

(iii)   establish an ECM information governance function and compliance framework;

(iv)   deliver the ECM strategy and programme;

(v)   create the ECM architecture and assess the major technology components.

Finally it discusses future trends in ECM.

6   ARCHITECTURE AND TECHNOLOGY

Architecture begins where engineering ends
Walter Gropius

Architecture is a representation of reality within a context of time, place and organisational culture. Architecture models represent how an organisation works and consider its current context to engender an understanding of the organisation's current vocabulary. They provide a view of the future working design through points of transition or transformation.

Architecture aims to make a technical solution or option for an organisation that fits in with common and emerging practice. Thus the investment delivers the returns, at least for the period recognised in the business case. Experienced architects tend to keep their options for the solution open, picking technology that is stable, proven and unlikely to change. They define which components of the solution rest within the organisation and which fall to outside partners to deliver. Good architecture is always about keeping options open. In the world of ECM, with its wide systems remit, this rule is particularly important.

This chapter discusses the following:

- the stakeholder challenge with a diverse portfolio of technology and a diverse enterprise set of stakeholders;
- some of the highlight technologies, where they have been and where they are going. It addresses not just legacy technologies but also how technology emerges and submerges in phases;
- the facets of service oriented architecture (SOA) and agile methods in the context of ECM;
- an in-depth case study of implementation and the lessons drawn from the approach.

STAKEHOLDER CHALLENGES

Creating viable software architecture requires the agreement of all stakeholders from both the business and technical communities. It demands a vision which can be shared and communicated at many different levels and from many different perspectives. Ultimately an architect must be a leader who can call on many allies within the organisation: a technical and considered sage, a decisive and persuasive advocate of the architecture.

The viability of the architecture is based on a number of valid representations and perspectives. Each imparts an idea to help understand the concepts of design. Each perspective on the architecture should be relevant to the stakeholder group to which it is presented and with which it has been agreed. It should offer the level of detail required to secure that group's commitment.

The challenge to the architect is to get agreement from each stakeholder. Often stakeholders wish to have more detailed perspectives than are appropriate for their levels of responsibility. This may simply be because they consider 'knowing it all' a useful means of managing risk without delegation. There are also those who feel that they need to belong to several peer groups.

The challenge is met by gathering stakeholders into similar categories of needs and building a matrix pack which recognise stakeholders' needs for components which meet their specific requirements. Once those groups are brought together they will need to have an appropriate level of influence or decision-making power. The key is then to build a similar decision set for each component.

AN ECM TECHNOLOGY REVIEW

Integration challenges

Most organisations in the early part of the 21st century are geared to working with numeric and structured data. This means that to categorise, file, or report on the progress or value of, their work is straightforward.

However over the past 25 years most systems integrators and software suppliers have focused on the relatively straightforward task of integrating structured data systems using databases. They have ignored the ever growing unstructured data piles which now exist in many organisations.

ECM started off storing large unstructured data in Binary Large Objects (BLOBs) in databases or in file systems. Its technology kept close to the infrastructure of the file and storage systems, using operating system services. These ran every time users updated, created or deleted files from the file system, whether on local, remote or network disk.

In the early days of client-server applications, the application services became centrally managed to co-ordinate read/write locks for the whole system. They encrypted the filename and the file for security and managed the submission to automated document publishing engines that would print and distribute it. They incorporated extensive process management engines to show whether organisations could keep pace with the amount of work moving through them.

Over the years document and content engines have stabilised to become commoditised, aiming to fit into the infrastructure of the organisation. After this development came the distribution complexity of cloud computing, prompting questions about ownership of assets and whether an organisation indeed needed to invest in its own storage.

The stumbling block today is that these applications have neglected the associated unstructured data that the business normally handles.

There are swathes of applications untouched by ECM offering an opportunity to make sense of the unstructured data:

For each of the applications in Table 6.1, decision making can be supplemented by access to the additional documents which were used as sources for the structured data. This may be a feature of compliance, which requires data changes to be backed up by the originating document.

Table 6.1

Application suite	Department	Application
ERP (enterprise resource planning)	HR	Policy and procedures
ERP	Legal	Contract management
ERP	Account	Invoice tracking
CRM (customer relationship management)	Customer support	Call centre help files; online forums
SCM (supply chain management)	Component tracking	Contracts management

The key to decision making is that we need supplementary information to support the structured data, which often does not contain enough context or information on which to base a decision. In this respect there was a need to re-engineer the backlog of applications quickly to extend their access to content.

Extending applications with smart forms
The opportunity for ECM is to integrate at infrastructure level or at the terminal without touching the application. This can be costly to adapt or maintain. Experience across a range of organisations has shown that application maintenance, especially managing data on the screen, is the most expensive form of integration maintenance within an organisation.

ECM vendors have concentrated on managing their customers by providing configurable electronic form systems which do not require code, and which integrate into business process systems to emulate sequential processors. Unfortunately even pseudo and high-level code still demands skills in logic and syntax to extend and provide linkage to forms and applications, as shown in Figure 6.1.To break into the application backlog a number of programming environments were developed which allowed federated content connector APIs to be shipped and used within any application development environment. The hope for the vendors was that developers and businesses would pick up the overall application technology.

Figure 6.1 Extending applications

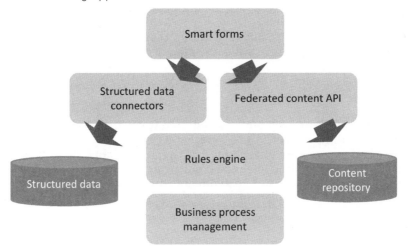

This approach had drawbacks, because the applications could rarely run in simple environments. They had to run in enterprise application environments such as Enterprise Java, with a significant amount of configuration and investment required to ensure the applications could run to scale. This was useful if momentum and economies of scale were sufficient for all applications to be delivered over the internet, something now only cloud and application service providers are likely to do, as corporations and organisations shrink and expand at rates demanded by the market.

If the organisation has specific expertise in development and marketing, it can piggyback on an industry specialist out of the cloud as many of the global organisations now consider insourcing their expertise back. The market for this approach is still open, as integrated development environments like Eclipse become open and syntactic language skills become merged.

ARCHITECTURES

Agile architectures

A good definition of software architecture is that it is something enabling an organisation to manage priorities as it evolves its technology infrastructure.

Decisions, relationships, and interactions are all encapsulated in a style or conceptual domain.

In the increasingly difficult and fluctuating environments in which organisations work, architectures need to be fluid. The challenge in acquiring a good definition is the push toward agile methodologies, which require non-formal iterative methods. However agile methodology is normally tightly bound and relatively small in scope: a micro-methodology within a micro-framework.

The conceptual scope of the software architecture may be considered macro in reach and definition but it provides the clarity and framework for agile methodologies to succeed. Agile methods require a framework defined by concepts, classes, patterns and metaphors. All of these are derived from the overall software architecture.

The challenge for most architects is to decide to what extent the software architecture definition needs to be detailed using criteria such as cost, criticality and extent. The underlying philosophy to adopt is: 'only do what is necessary'. The overarching lesson in creating agile architecture is to keep it as conceptual as possible and use components which provide basic, loosely coupled connectivity and control.

Finding a framework

There are several architectural frameworks through which ECM can be delivered:

SOAs (service oriented architectures)-: Delivering a set of services if there is a connectivity bus for loosely coupled messaging-based services.

Enterprise environment: Building a set of application EJBs that provide a tightly coupled enterprise application – mentioned earlier in the integration discussion – but delivered by service providers for outsourced environments.

Value-added bespoke: Delivering a single-client application if there are many divisions operating in different sectors with common products, possibly with open source products.

COTS (Commercial Off-The-Shelf) Applications: Delivering a common acquisition technology which means very simple forms of integration, through either service providers, over the cloud, or heap packages.

Architects should consider the matrix in which these frameworks provide flexibility and cost. The ideal, in the SOA quadrant, is owner-controlled flexible response. The transition to the quadrant is dependent on the starting point, as illustrated in Figure 6.2.

COTS packages, although relatively cheap or even free, may be not as effective. They have deliberate mass product acceptance which does not allow them to be

Figure 6.2 Comparison of application frameworks

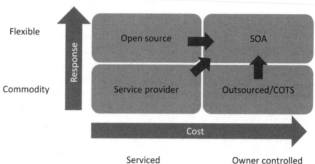

customised without the risk that the customisation might become unsupportable when a new release appears.

Organisations may have already outsourced their applications and environments. However by doing so they have recognised that the development of these applications is now out of their reach, as it is likely that development resources have also moved on.

Open source products are useful and inexpensive to rollout. However they necessitate training in the use of new applications and environments such as PHP or Linux.

Service providers supplying services and applications through the internet have a lower expectation of cross-integration. Therefore they will need to meet all the needs of the organisation, including those for content.

With the advent of new infrastructures and distributed architectures, some vendors emphasise the need for standards. However they usually tend to promote a single core generic enterprise platforms standard. Open standards and the use of open source would be a recommended approach if the skills were available to maintain the necessary level of flexibility.

SERVICE ORIENTED ARCHITECTURE

Service oriented architecture is a fundamental step forward in agile integration. It requires significant investment in a framework architecture for running the services, however. The benefits of adopting an SOA are improved availability, maintainability, reliability and interoperability of applications alongside lower operating and development costs.

One of the key trends and challenges in ECM, mentioned earlier, is integrating a diverse set of legacy applications which are traditionally in place across the organisation.

Functional encapsulation into objects, and the definition or publication of interfaces, are key to integration, with SOA defining the organisation and management of those objects. SOA relies on the loosely coupled management of services with consumer applications. This separation enables better control of change at a technical level, which results in an improved ability to respond to changes in markets.

Having uniform access to all the information assets is key in ECM, and the management of common services provides valuable integration benefits. The architect must ensure that a vendor has embraced the SOA components necessary for continuous innovation and integration.

SOA – the agile framework

Like ECM, SOA uses a catalogue or directory of services. These can be selected through open integrated development environments (IDEs) like Eclipse, with code automation to enable connection to the service as required. It can also provide dynamic proxies which can enable connection at runtime.

The lack of dependency between the architecture layers in SOA helps reduce development and maintenance risks, and enhance rapid application development practice. The adoption of SOA will continue to provide benefits to the organisation during the development and configuration of its business applications.

This loosely coupled environment helps an organisation in constant flux to manage its evolution. Legacy applications are relatively straightforward to encapsulate through services extending their lives with little investment, but also ensure enterprise-wide integration of core resources and applications.

SOA – benefits

There are several benefits linked to SOA methods:

- The customisation of the presentation layer is partitioned better.
- Mature services, quickly deployed, can be incrementally improved, tested and extended with only a need to regression test.
- ECM systems and implementations consistently rely on an infrastructure built on SOA.

SOA provides the intrinsically difficult aspects of integration between components: namely transport, business logic, resources and access management. The loose coupling enables the ring-fencing of new components and services with the extension of test probe and communication scenario services to assure the integration.

SOA – characteristics

SOA has some key characteristics important to ECM implementations. It is important to remember that web services, a common form of object integration, is just one implementation of SOA. Some ECM product suites provide a set of subsidiary web services which can be incorporated into an SOA framework, but it is rare for ECM suites to provide such a framework.

The contract is central to the concept of SOA. Like any other business contract, it is made up of a definition of the interfaces and services provided. These are published through the SOA directory. They allow all consumer applications to connect to the service, as they provide a standard description of interaction or binding with the service.

Modern object-based applications tend to be built around classes in which functions are hierarchically managed but tightly bound – with each child reliant on the parent class – and organised with a high level of interdependency. Services complement this tight binding through the loose binding of the directory of services, like interfaces to extend the application.

Application interfaces usually provide information on the form of the data retrieved, the request format and error messages provided through an interface definition language (IDL). SOA interfaces extend this language by providing session context such as pre- and post-conditions and optional quality of service metrics. There are two types of interface: technical and business. The business interface usually extends the idea of quality of service metrics in terms of security, availability, reliability and exception policies.

SOA – data access

One of the key components used in ECM is the process of gathering data from structured or unstructured repositories which are not part of the core repository. Often there is a need to extend reporting capability, especially in financial systems, by gathering more data and presenting them in a different or consolidated format.

A number of services enable snippets of content to be generated specifically for the presentation layer most appropriate to the consumer application. These include HTML and XML, for report generators) and PDF, for consolidated report sheets.

One of the considerable challenges for the business community in a highly regulated environment is to achieve information movement encapsulating information on source, system and auditable unique identifiers. This means it can be traced. An ECM system using such a service will often provide this level of functionality. It treats a record, or a set of records, of information and its presentation as a piece of content which can readily be stored and retrieved across the organisation.

ECM SERVICE COMPONENTS

The following components as shown in Figure 6.3, make up a typical ECM vendor suite.

- distribution channels:
  - encompassing applications and generic application interfaces;
- performance management:
  - (a) business intelligence and reporting;
  - (b) business process management for workflows, business rules for distribution and reference;

- information management:
  - (a) storage/databases/directories: organisation of content object storage;
  - (b) content control: annotations, comments, processing search vocabularies/taxonomy: how meaning is organised or specialised;
  - (c) search catalogues: caches of current search decompositions;
  - (d) content model: how content is interrelated from a business perspective, including the extension of attributes for each class of content object;
  - (e) audit/lifecycle/records: how audit is managed, how records are generated andhow the lifecycle remains coherent for retention;

- Infrastructure:
  - (a) security model: how security is aligned to content and users;
  - (b) integration model: web services, authentication, EJB, as a library within the code, tightly coupled and integrated, or localised within the local operating system.

CASE STUDY: FINANCE INDUSTRY

This extensive case study reflects first-hand lessons from the adoption of a very capable ECM technology regarded as one of the market leaders. Even with all this recognised leadership in technology and management, the road to delivery was not smooth.

Test non-core capability

All technology suppliers develop new bolt-on services or acquire new companies to make delivery to market an effective large suite of applications. No matter how mature applications, especially ECM applications, can be extremely wide in scope and capability. Often they are cobbled together from different vendors over an extended period as the ability of the software industry to respond to demand or innovate fluctuates.

Figure 6.3 Services framework

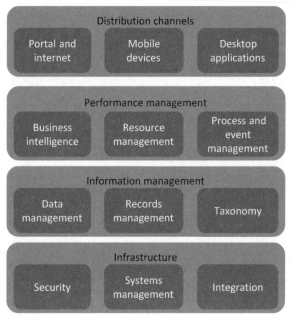

It is important to understand and test the capability of the peripheral technology early on. For example file replication needs to be tested so that one can assess whether the technology is as rugged as the core architecture. In the case of file replication the complexity of determining the master and slave documents meant that, over the period of the project, it would have been difficult to manage and move document repositories to other remote locations.

It was a good decision **not** to use the replication service at that time. Network storage technology had adapted to include low-level and infrastructure level synchronisation of data across storage components for live and disaster recovery operations.

Other peripheral applications and services may not be available in other system solutions.

Document types

One of the surprises for a project of this length is the emergence of a certain document type within the system. There was an initial model for capacity: 50 per cent of documents would be scanned, with only 10 per cent being email, the rest being mopped up by PDF generation. This changed dramatically, simply because of the trend within the industry as it moved away from paper systems.

Today there are new media for capture. For example Twitter and Facebook were made possible by managing document types and their classification.

In terms of capacity, automated PDF capture of statements represented 50 per cent, with 40 per cent taken up with email and attachments.

Electronic documents generated from the desktop using traditional methods rarely show in the productivity of an organisation. It is important, therefore, to determine which applications are used most every day, i.e. email. It is likewise important to establish which automated capture processes facilitate document generation, and what the traffic for usual operation is, i.e. printer spool to a PDF generator.

Federated search and niche players

Carry out fundamental tests on federated search components long before adopting them. Where sophisticated technology is concerned, large companies swallow up some small niche companies which provide such essential services.

In the end the niche technology was a very useful addition to the larger companies' technology stack. Beware, however, that support may shift to a lower level of service, as the new owner may not have apprised its sales or integration teams of the benefits of using and developing with the hot piece of technology. The large company may even start to sell the organisation something else or just kill the new acquisition to maintain its market and technology share.

Some suppliers provide their own search content catalogues in direct competition to such product specialists such as Google. Often adopting the best of breed is more effective in the case of core search technologies. The use of prototypes is recommended, to prove that the development roadmap is accurate.

Certain technologies have phases of development shifting from innovative but risky to solid but non-competitive. Protect the organisation by appreciating what risk it is likely to accept in return for an opportunity to gain market share with unique functionality.

Middleware

Many software vendors provide OEM (original equipment manufacturer) solutions for managing the archiving of documents between magnetic storage and optical disks. As these get swallowed up by competitors, it may be prudent to find a dual-sourcing methodology at the start so that there are no technical shocks along the way. Keep the architecture as loosely coupled as possible during the programme of work so that changes can be managed over time.

Network capacity

The architect should be prepared to run several performance tools to optimise the application and service builds. Intelligent network monitoring products are able to profile applications and determine where the bottlenecks will be without scaling to large load tests. Intelligent monitors are useful because they can understand the demographics of SQL calls on the network. Be aware that many ECM products protect their core capability in the database with encrypted procedures and scripts, rather than plain open SQL calls through the API.

Network monitoring tools will pinpoint real issues with any thick client- or web-based applications and determine some of the key points to address when building an internet delivery system. It will be found that most of the document movement operations tend to converge into back-end web services and messaging. These are based on a selection of MQSeries and basic JMS queues handled by listener applications, for example, if the environment is based on EJBs.

Real advantages will be seen when the organisation starts to commoditise the programme of work. This involves outsourcing parts of its back-end financial systems to another country as the application is already working through the internet.

Process engines

A workflow or process management system will require upgrading. Process engines are notoriously difficult to manage through transition, as the system maintains real-time queues which manage the critical aspects of the organisation's processes. One lost or re-diverted transaction badly placed could mean significant losses for the organisation.

Practice building processes and changing them so that they have natural end points for migration. This allows process migration and upgrades without bringing the whole audit system down. Practice makes perfect and for in-stream business operations it will not be possible to have downtime and process generation or stoppages in migration.

Workflow systems need rugged and solid process systems. If performance is likely to be affected because of a memory or data leak, then be very aware of how to avoid increases in process queues without sacrificing logging and audit traces. Most workflow and business process vendors should be able to provide capacity management estimates for sizing the environment. We should determine what is useful in the metrics of the system and set the expectations according to the amount of log storage for tracking workflows in action.

Search capability

In the searching and definition of a taxonomy, discussed in a later chapter, the level of search performance is driven by the number of properties in a document class. In analysis the number of numeric key identifiers for the enterprise should be kept to around 5 to 10 so as not to stretch the database technology too far. Database technology is good for transaction-based systems but is not necessarily effective with millions of records on which to build process status reports on the fly.

It may be very tempting to have lots of index terms. Sometimes as many as 100 are used, but the indexing of these will seriously hinder performance. If we consider the third stage of the content maturity model, the enterprise should be aware of its most important identifier. Organisations not at this level will give in to the mavericks who insist on having their parts of the business represented by their own terms and attributes.

When searching complex terms the system may need a supplementary RDBMS solution – very much like reporting – to enable the simpler and quicker searching of documents which previously required too many terms to find. This can divert the processing capacity for searching so that document acquisition performance is not affected.

Storage management

It may be found that the system is so successful that capacity plans have to be drawn up to manage the growth of storage. In the process it may be possible to start switching to new volume management systems which allow flexible allocation of capacity to volumes. Luckily the storage systems were innovating quickly in this case, but this is not always true.

Less is more: it is better to qualify the documents that are deemed useful to the business and to set the entry level high enough to keep the management of such documents clean. For all other document types use a different storage, archive and protection scheme based on email or file systems, for example.

SUMMARY

A number of lessons were learnt in this assignment. All of these can be generically considered in ECM projects:

- Test non-core capability which has not been long-established or seems unusual in the ECM portfolio of functions.

- Be surprised at the estimates of what document types the organisation captures and works with.

- Be aware of the advantages and disadvantages of picking niche technology.

- Avoid the technical dependency shock by finding dual sources or alternative solutions early on.

- Start to really understand the transactions on the network. Network capacity makes a difference for worldwide operations and outsourcing. This becomes more relevant when considering capacity for the large number of users which some systems are exposed to.

- Managing process engines through transition is not straightforward.

- Content attribute searches can be severely affected by the number of attributes for a set of document classes.

- Ensure that there is a good document retention policy in place to manage storage.

7   STORAGE

Fifteen cents in every twenty-cent stamp goes to storage
Louis Rukeyser

Storage is important because it has to be flexible to grow and work with increasing levels of partitioning and distribution. Data volumes are growing every year by 40–75 per cent. Unstructured data such as email, presentations, reports and video are growing by more than 90 per cent annually.

As the global economies expand and the highly distributed global corporations consolidate and transact business, structured transaction data growth will be far more volatile and dependent on regional economies. This volatility will not apply to content and unstructured data.

Organisations face a number of challenges in growth. These provide a compelling argument for establishing a strategic approach to storage management:

- increasing exponential volumes;
- decreasing budgets;
- increasing retention and availability requirements.

The typical response by less informed IT services is simply to add primary storage. This ultimately makes the cost of storage and its maintenance far outweigh its possible value. Taking the view that information has a lifecycle is a significant aid to streamlining and optimising the management of storage. 80 per cent of storage managers admit that they simply purchase more storage rather than investigate ways of getting more from their resources.

BUSINESS ALIGNMENT

Storage management requires an understanding of the business definition of data to enable further levels of management flexibility. In the past, without this decomposition into layers, a single solution to fit all circumstances used to be built at a high overall cost. With different storage tiers in place, some of that cost can now be moved to the management of storage and the maintenance of a number of suppliers of storage, together with differing systems. However as the storage requirements grow, the cost of management tends to escalate as much as the cost of adopting a single storage system.

INCREASING CAPACITY

Before increasing the capacity of any storage system, an assessment of the level of capacity optimisation needs to take place. Some optimisation measures can be taken:

- classifying data to ensure that they reside in the correct class or archive;
- eliminating unnecessary copies;
- moving less important data to less expensive storage media;
- reallocating unused capacity.

This should result in a significant reduction in hardware and management costs.

It is also important to have resource restrictions. Hence users and organisations can understand the capacity use of storage made available to them and the implications of not managing it.

MANAGING TIERS OF STORAGE

By organising storage into tiers an organisation can allocate specific tiers with different combinations of the following characteristics:

- cost: lowering cost of total ownership of data per terabyte;
- security: complying with regulations based on the need for 'legal hold' or data protection;
- retention: complying with retention regulations;
- performance: where systems demand;
- accessibility: meeting the needs of the ownership rights.

This depends on whether the organisation has a set of different storage media (solid state, disc, tape or optical).

A plan of action in terms of organising storage by tiers means that hardware, data placement, applications and systems access have to be assessed. Even small and seemingly insignificant data, although straightforward to store, can have a significant effect on an organisation.

The storage tiers should be identified during the creation of the file plan (discussed in a later chapter).

Exercising migrating data is an important aspect of content management. Organisations which practice migration and transformation of documents into new optimised locations with the same frequency and rigour of disaster recovery become more flexible. Software solutions which provide constant document optimisation out of the box are good candidates. Now that organisations are intermittently connected through the internet and content is viewed constantly, internal storage components and systems need to be engaged in constant background change. This need is similar to that for online backups.

VALUING DATA

A simple mantra should be: 'old data has less value than new data.' Research has suggested that the chances of unstructured data being accessed after 90 days from its creation are close to 0 per cent.

One of the factors in understanding the value of data is the awareness of the cost of storage that the organisation gains by allocating its needs into tiers of capability: retention, capacity, security, accessibility and resilience. Once it has done this, and an outsourced or cloud cost is established, the future cost will be far clearer. Add to this the fact that storage can now exist outside the organisation, through the cloud or outsourced organisations, and the costs become far more transparent.

STORAGE MEDIUM

The medium on which data is stored provides various levels of read/write access, longevity and security. In the past volatile, working and fast memory required power, so was unlikely to be useful as a long-term store, especially in the light of the increasing cost of power. For memory, there is now a burgeoning variety of solid-state FLASH technologies which have low power consumption with less mechanical power, and generate less concomitant heat.

Hard disks have consistently reduced in size and increased in capacity, bringing the price per gigabyte down. Manufacturers have had to create more sophisticated control mechanisms to sustain that growth. Often these are expressed as enterprise devices, which improve power performance and provide failure diagnostic and sector management, such as SMART+, to push the physical and logical boundaries of the technology to the edge of their operational scope.

As with all technology, the more sophisticated it becomes, the more fragile its operation is. Much more care needs to be taken with the disk operating environment, with the two fundamental considerations being temperature and power. Some environments require strict conditioning of air to ensure disk arrays can sustain the optimum temperature.

Power variations, failures and spikes occur in the supply, so protecting the equipment with suppression and cleaning devices is imperative. A simple experiment is to compare the number of enterprise-class internal disk errors over a three-month period when the disk is connected to a normal mains supply to that when it is powered through a clean supply battery-backed system.

STORAGE TECHNOLOGIES

Table 7.1 illustrates the comparative costs for storage:

Table 7.1

Storage technology	Cost in US cents per gigabyte (2010)
Enterprise disk (FC, SCSI, FICON, ESCON)	50–70
Mid-range disk (SCSI, FC)	20–35
Low cost disk (SATA II, JBODs)	5–15
Automated tape	1–4
Optical media	2–10

Some of the most common disk architectures are those in the SATA II class.

SATA, known now as SATA II as it includes higher data transfer rates, has become a commodity in pricing and performance. However there are some key considerations when using it:

- SATA is not a total solution to storage growth. Just because it is cheap and fast does not mean that it is any easier to add to the current storage solutions. It cannot solve a business process problem, like runaway storage growth. In the long run, it will make things worse unless a new storage management approach is adopted.

- SATA should not be used everywhere. SATA is neither SCSI nor ATA. The application should be considered and the drive technology matched to it. It is possible to replace SATA drives with SAS drives which connect on the same backplane, if need be. SAS will also support 16,000 drives on a single backplane connection.

- Replacing several drives with a higher capacity drive should only be considered as a last resort. There could be an unacceptable performance hit, as more spindles do not necessarily mean better performance with stripping. The reason that SATA can come bigger than SAS and SCSI drives is that it has slower rotation speeds with a resultant reduction in data transfer rates.

STORAGE REPOSITORIES

The repository is a central component in ECM. ECM repositories vary in size and complexity, depending on the technologies used to create them. Storage can exist in different forms: magnetic hard disk, memory, tape, optical disk, microfilm and paper. It can also exist in different configurations, cloud-accessed, server-attached, network-attached, and network arrays, each with its own advantages and costs.

Another aspect of managing costs is to provide a storage profile which puts content online or through a cloud service for immediate and fast access – when opening the document for viewing or streaming as if it were being viewed on a local device – or near-line for download-type performance of approximately 30 seconds –when downloading a document from the internet before viewing – or offline or in an archive for content which can be viewed physically – like paper and microfilm – in the store but still referenced through an online index. The business model and the demands of the stakeholders will determine which of these options is chosen.

Storage performance is a factor in ECM because data can be structured and unstructured, with the two often being coincident. An unstructured file or image of a document is stored in contiguous blocks, while the index entry indicating the attributes of that file also needs to be kept in a structured storage configuration, such as a database.

Some ECM technologies allow the storage of these two components in one repository. These store the unstructured data in a BLOB as a special or extended data type in a database. This requires the database to manage the extended data types in its own file-space. Therefore it relies on off-the-shelf database technology to deal with the large and extensive storage demands of the user base. Such technology is able to carry out contiguous live data backup and recovery on file space as well as database volumes.

Other technologies use their own data storage code to manage the storage of the file separately from the structured data. Usually these rely on off-the-shelf databases, to manage the simple indexed entries, and investment in the generic technology, to resolve issues of performance. Simplicity is sacrificed to optimise the recovery of different forms of storage.

Content has a concept of timeliness: hence the emphasis on timing within organisational analysis in the business guide. Some content, such as stock figures, needs to be accessed quickly but is irrelevant the next day when it is superseded. It can be maintained for historic purposes so that stock can be analysed to assess trends over seasons. There is also content which may need to be kept over decades: that which might have a historic interest or legislative context.

We also need to consider that, as technologies change, migration to newer, cheaper, sustainable storage media will need to be catered for. The mechanism for such document management already exists in the scan centre when paper is transformed into electronic images. It may even be viable to consider micro-fiches as a sustainable long-term, low-carbon footprint approach to image storage. Micro-fiches can also store binary images, for example through two-dimensional bar coding technologies.

Backups of content can exist either as duplicates in the same medium or in a different one. Economies of scale and distribution are gained through using the same medium, such as magnetic disk over network-attached storage (NAS). However when transformation is required, an additional cost is incurred to move between the two forms and maintain them. For examplea tape library system is required to maintain the link between magnetic hard disk and tapes.

Backups concern the protection and availability of content or information. Continuity concerns the resilience of business operations, with the backup strategy playing an important part.

Configurations

The configurations for storage vary to allow either central or distributed control of storage media. There are configurations for managing differing access rights. These are usually a means of managing the safe provision of files from a separate public repository. This means that there is duplication of hardware and storage for the simple expedient of securing access rights. Management overheads also increase. A good solution should recognise that it is not the placement of the data in a separate area but the availability of a service to manage public access which provides true protection. The way that service is published should mean that any public access identities should only have access to public-level services.

Federated data storage

A federation is defined as a number of independent systems but with a single governing process. Over the years organisations have created and acquired various and numerous repositories and technologies, each managing a different retention and disposal method. To avoid the expense and disruption of moving records and amending their respective applications into a single repository, a federated approach can be taken.

The essence of content federation is that a single interface is made available to enable access to a plethora of content repositories. These are interconnected in such a way that they can act with common functions.

Normally a place-holder or object reference is stored in a catalogue, similarly to how search services would store it, through which an external or federated piece of content can be referenced. The object reference still manages the metadata concerned with the content, ultimately because databases themselves are not federated.

The issue with managing federated content is that organisations rely on the federation process. It allows them to remain stable and continue to access the vast array of repositories whilst maintaining the required integrity of content, without loss of acuity or traceability of change.

In terms of fail-safe mechanisms, there are solutions such as providing encrypted packets which are also stored on the external repository so that a link back remains to the original store. Should the local system fail, the remote content can still be found because it has these associated lightweight tags.

Each storage repository has basic characteristics – time of creation, size and so forth – which form some of the metadata for a document. Other characteristics specific to a business are not inherent in the remote repository and so should be stored as extended attributes.

Instead of a federated system, and to counter the inability of the middleware to have full retention and disposal control, some systems manage the document in its original context by copying it into a managed storage environment especially for documents, such as an archive, replacing the original with a stub or smart short cut. The stub is then managed as a place-holder which redirects enquiries from the original context or library to the managed store. This may simply be a competitive and different approach to managing the documents: to lock the organisation into using a single record management technology, rather than working with the constant flexibility of a federated storage system.

The advantage of using the federated approach is that the open interface should allow any organisation with the development means to construct and maintain interfaces to any application. From an architectural perspective, knowing who owns and maintains federated interfaces is important. Keeping the interfaces open is key to retaining long-term investment. They should always be subject to ESCROW agreements, especially where there is a commercial degradation of service if the supplier is bought up.

Storage architectures
In 2009 monolithic enterprise storage increased globally by 25 per cent per annum, modular storage by 50 per cent and low-cost capacity storage by 80 per cent. Within 5 years there will be 34 times more storage capacity to manage. Utilisation of directed attached storage (DAS) rarely exceeds 50 per cent yet, with proper storage management, this could increase to 70–90 per cent.

Storage networking
Before storage networking, computing environments used internal or directly connected storage, i.e. storage ostensibly controlled within the processing environment. Sun Microsystems Inc. developed the network file system (NFS) for UNIX to allow the sharing and use of data files over a TCP/IP network, but with all characteristics of performance suggesting they were stored locally. Microsoft in turn created the server message block (SMB) protocol to do the same with Windows computers, and later renamed it the common internet file system (CIFS).

Network attached storage
It has long been recognised that layering is an excellent engineering mechanism to break down and optimise the processes for carrying out operations. The computer server, centred on the CPU, meant that the CPU was

designed to manage a multiplicity of operations. That it could do many different things did not mean that a server should be built to do so. There are now specialist appliances which do just one thing very well. This becomes very useful where elements of a system, like storage, have commodity status, either through the sheer demand for storage or its low incremental cost.

Network-attached storage (NAS) facilitates the attachment of a storage appliance directly to a TCP/IP network. It is simply optimised for managing cache and I/O whilst leaving the functions of an application or processing server to a separate device. It enables users to access storage capacity using CIFS or NFS with an asynchronous protocol.

NAS works best for the following types of application:

- file serving;
- file sharing;
- users' home directories;
- content archiving;
- metadata directories;
- email repositories, such as enterprise .PST files;
- GRID computing (using high-bandwidth networks);
- Peer-to-peer data sharing.

However NAS, in its most recent incarnation, can replace SAN or DAS. The caching components, in combination with the high gigabit bandwidth networks using Jumbo frames over fibre, can emulate the performance possible with direct attached servers used for databases.

NAS considerations
As CIFS and NFS are strictly asynchronous protocols of TCP/IP, the reliability, connectivity and performance of the network become important when resolving issues. NAS storage appliances can be configured to serve both UNIX and Windows clients by running both protocols at once. NAS has also adopted some of the plug-and-go approaches to DAS disk management in RAID, by enabling self-synchronisation to other NAS appliances.

Connectivity
The NAS product should be connected to at least two IP switches and the product should be configured as a cluster, so that a switch failure or NAS head failure does not affect client connectivity. Popular appliances can take advantage of virtual interfaces which allow almost transparent failover to another IP port if one port or path goes down.

Hardware

The underlying disks used for the NAS storage can dramatically affect performance. Use hardware-based RAID-protected storage for best availability and performance, since software-based RAID can cause performance issues during disk failures. Spread network cards across PCI buses within the server to prevent internal bottlenecks.

Migration

Some NAS appliances allow the creation of virtual servers for representing NAS shares. Using virtual servers simplifies the migration to an NAS appliance, since each can mimic the node name and IP address of the server it is replacing. If using a Linux-based appliance for Windows CIFS shares, make sure that the latest versions of software patches are used to reduce issues of incompatibility.

Network

NAS performance can be an issue when supporting many simultaneous clients. Ensure that the network supports Virtual LANs (VLANs), for traffic isolation, and IP trunks or port channelling, for better bandwidth allocation and aggregation. Currently gigabit Ethernet is the best platform for NAS shares, as it provides the most robust bandwidth. It should also use jumbo frames where possible to increase performance for large file transfers.

Security

Optical networks are more secure than copper networks, since the cables are more difficult to tap. The backbone of the NAS infrastructure should use optical connections. When implementing a security model for files over NAS that will be shared between UNIX and Windows clients, make sure the NAS server can apply UNIX-style security. It should also be integrated with Windows ACL security and Active Directory.

Storage array network

With internal storage or DAS it is difficult to allow another processor to share the storage using the SCSI interface – the high-speed bus system that interconnects the sub-systems of a computer. To improve performance in the accessing of storage, the network used for storage array networks (SAN) was developed with very low latency, high reliability, high bandwidth and synchronous communication. High-bandwidth optical cables were used with the Fibre Channel protocol to allow shared access into the SCSI interface.

This led to having centralised storage systems, accessed using Fibre Channel to multiple computers, and the extension of capacity clustering. These low-latency networks allow large blocks of data to move very fast from processor to storage.

SAN works best for any application which requires low latency and high bandwidth for data movement:

- databases;
- server clustering;
- messaging applications;
- backup;
- data replication;
- GRID computing
- data warehousing;
- recovery archives.

There has always been contention between the two approaches for dominance of the storage market. For example, iSCSI has effectively extended CIFS and NFS protocols to work with a generic block-level protocol rather than a file-level one.

SUMMARY

This chapter has discussed issues of storage, configurations and their technologies.

8 MANAGING CHANGE

To improve is to change; to be perfect is to change often
Winston Churchill

How do we manage the transformation of information in our organisation? How do we change the culture of our organisation so that it accepts constant flux as part of the natural order? To answer these questions we must appreciate how concepts are represented and what drives us to create and contribute to them. We will then look at our position in the organisation and see what organisations can do to harness our need to create by encouraging a sharing culture.

REPRESENTATIONS TO CONCEPTS

Information is a representation of perspectives. Often it is a single interpretation from an author, artist or a director, together with that person's team.

Information is not knowledge. We have many forms of representation but no simple representation of concepts or knowledge: one that is non-contextual, universally understood and applicable across a number of disciplines. There is still a significant gap between a simple or complex representation and the idea of a concept or knowledge, as illustrated in Figure 8.1.

Information and its representation can have a range of forms, from simple static data to complex and dynamic video and sounds. It can also contain a number of perspectives. The larger the number, the more effective the information is in decision making and the more useful it is conceptually.

Concepts can be complex, persist over time, be accumulative and impress from multiple perspectives, very much like philosophy and culture. The rich tapestry in which concepts are woven is some way from the shallow capture of words, pictures and moving images on which the information society is based today.

There are many layers of knowledge, exhaustive opinions and consultations which can take years to master, machinate and accumulate. It will become increasingly difficult to accumulate conceptual knowledge, as there is a danger of repeating mistakes or ignoring previous research, records of which have long been inaccessible, lost, or forgotten. The challenge for an information society is to accumulate conceptual knowledge in a cohesive and transparent manner.

We will now look at how ideas are created and sustained, the information culture and how to instil awareness of the need for sharing.

Figure 8.1 Representation to conceptual gap

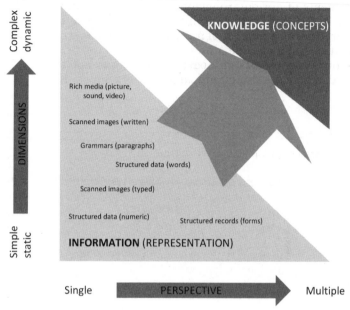

Complex dynamic

DIMENSIONS

Simple static

KNOWLEDGE (CONCEPTS)

Rich media (picture, sound, video)

Scanned images (written)

Grammars (paragraphs)

Structured data (words)

Scanned images (typed)

Structured data (numeric)

Structured records (forms)

INFORMATION (REPRESENTATION)

Single — PERSPECTIVE — Multiple

THE CREATION OF IDEAS

Information is the cauldron or human soup in which we manifest new ideas. From birth we discover the world by interacting with it and remember the elements of cause and effect on our physical being. From school we learn sets of rules in a number of disciplines from books, quickly acquiring basic knowledge. Through college we test that knowledge by extending our intellectual psyche. As we join organisations we become parts of teams in which our differing perspectives and experiences come together to build and deliver ideas to sustain organisations and make them grow: our social psyche.

The journey through our world starts with the conceptual plane. The concept moves into physical realities that over time come to be appreciated as objects of antiquity and experience, which become highly valued and rare.

Thoughts do not persist unless they can leap into the physical and by doing so acquire an increase in value by an order of magnitude. As physical objects which are appreciated for their beauty or historic context, they leap into the realm of human antiquity, increasing in value as they become rarer.

Concepts and objects which do not make that leap simply do not persist. ECM manages the conceptual pool through which collaboration and change can manage the delivery into physical reality.

Collaboration, and leaping from the conceptual pool into reality, is a journey of transformation, as Figure 8.2 demonstrates. We quickly assimilate trends in and measurements of our environments and the market sectors in which our organisations exist. With this basic information we write reports or consider analysis incorporating a number of perspectives to focus on a particular facet of our investigations. We provide a number of rich contexts and representations to persuade our counterparts of a particular issue or opportunity, together building an idea which has a significant level of support information.

Figure 8.2 Concept evolution

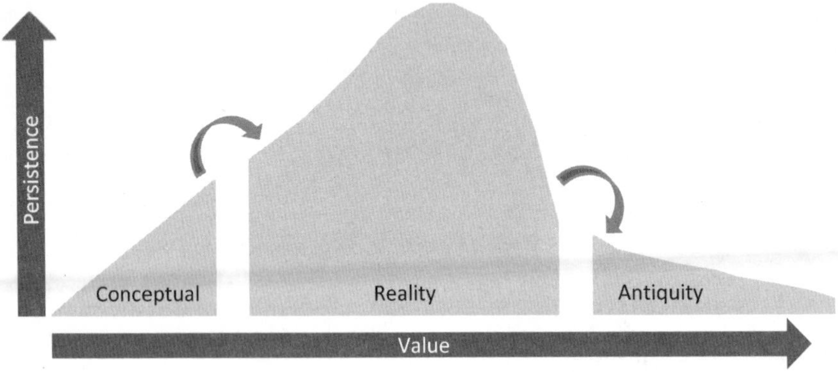

The organisation turns the ideas into reality. Ideas are placed in the organisation or further still into society and create a reaction or stimulus which in turn creates information for the conceptual pool. This allows the next analyst to investigate and recreate the next evolutionary and progressive step.

Reality has tangible value whereas the conceptual pool does not. Information is valuable if it can persist to create and sustain ideas. In principle information needs to be shared, open and perceptive to persist.

Let us now see how ECM can manage the leap from the conceptual plane, engage stakeholders and change behaviours in an organisation by looking at these principles.

Sharing information
The dated dictum 'knowledge is power' still permeates many organisations today. It is not the prime reason knowledge is not shared but it is a factor. People have a stake in how they have acquired their knowledge and experience. They are naturally reticent to share it unless the organisation can provide the means by which they can see it published and acknowledged.

To address the lack of motivation to share, organisations need to emphasise 'teamwork' and the collective process. Knowledge grows with collaboration. Few people have all the knowledge on a subject because knowledge has an experiential component. Individual experience is not universal, so cannot be complete. Therefore knowledge has to be based on the cumulative experience of a number of practitioners, who come together to create a 'book of knowledge' for universal use.

Those who feel their own knowledge is sufficient are often led into a false sense of security about its efficacy. Individuals should recognise that knowledge, and the information on which it is based, need to be maintained and that, more important, they degrade over time.

Open information
No employee or member of an organisation should have exclusive access to valuable information and knowledge. Should such a case occur then this would draw attention to issues of information governance and, if such information were transactional and specific to a regulated market, it would also be non-compliant. As parts of the information governance process, secrets should be encapsulated into patentable products wherever possible. Contracts which prevent knowledge being divulged for a certain period after employment termination are largely unenforceable as former employees can use the knowledge rather than divulge it.

Contestable information
Some accumulated information and knowledge is not supported by any understanding. Organisations should always try to ask people within organisations 'why?' rather than 'what?' In the ECM model motivation and value are added from the management perspective and not necessarily from the content one.

Learning experience
Human endeavour is a voyage of discovery on roads well trod. Many employees consider this voyage an essential part of learning. Some may consider collaborative knowledge less powerful than that gathered alone. Yet when we consider that some of the best and most enduring business relationships have taken place in partnerships, for instance Gates and Jobs or Hewlett and Packard, we see that having a bouncing board is the most productive, and often the most effective way, of building knowledge.

Knowledge is all about the context of information. The significance of information that some people have may not be understood except through others' eyes. Some information can be a useful trigger for new ideas and innovations. As suggested before, innovation across disciplines or perspectives bears fruit.

There is a disconnection between corporate and personal knowledge which is only resolved by the building of trust. Such trust allows a person to cede information and knowledge to the corporation. The key to managing this is to acknowledge the information, but also to understand that its use is backed by context. There is a large difference between coming up with ideas and making them work. Neither should be reliant on the other where recognition is concerned. People should be recognised separately for the idea and for its execution: both facets of innovation are important. When things go wrong in delivery those responsible for the ideas do not get disheartened by the machinations of commercial or political idiosyncrasies. They should still be able to create ideas, and the managers should work out another means to deliver these. In order to have an organisation which manages its creativity and delivery we need to recognise that employees take different roles throughout their work.

CHANGING ROLES

We don't send our books and reference material to school: we send ourselves to school. We are the mechanisms for acquiring knowledge, not catalogues or encyclopaedias. When time is of the essence, having the right people with the right knowledge can be seen as more important than having recorded information. However there should be a process which allows knowledge to be shared on a periodic basis with those that don't have it.

If we apply the ECM model for acquisition, storage and delivery to the changing roles of employees as they work with information, we see a correlation in the actions necessary for employees to work in an ECM environment.

People have a multiplicity of roles, as shown in Figure 8.3. These form a cycle of learning, practice and teaching that should continue throughout their working

---

Figure 8.3 Information roles

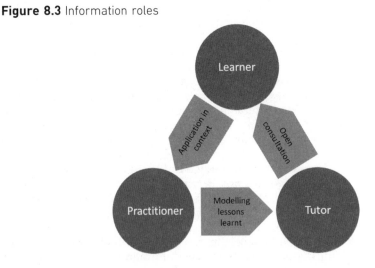

lives. Businesses have traditionally considered themselves to be all about practice, albeit with a grudging acknowledgement of the need for training. Rarely are employees given the opportunity to teach.

Fundamentally businesses demand learning skills from their employees. This is a major factor in organisations employing graduates, which is done not because of what they know, but because they have been taught how to manage constant and self-motivated learning. Organisations also demand information systems skills, such as the ability to work with a word processor or a spreadsheet, as well as some language and social skills in order to communicate effectively.

However tomorrow's organisations will demand that their employees take communication to the next level and become tutors of the knowledge and information, thus sharing their experiences. If organisations were to think of their employees as learners, practitioners and tutors, they would be in a better position to maintain their cultures and information. This would mean that, as practitioners finish projects, they build a course of learning based on their experience, for example lessons learnt.

Some organisations already build collateral or case studies on what has gone before, with the aim of promoting the achievements of the organisation. However these case studies are usually the preserve of the marketing department specialists. The opportunity rests with organisations that can break the mould by having their practitioners practice the promotional aspects. It is the practitioners now networking at conferences, sales meetings or webinars who need to be fully conversant with their organisations' products.

MANAGING CULTURAL CHANGE

We have seen that there are some fundamentals in addressing people and culture: reward, trust through commitment and collaborative teams. There is neither a straightforward nor a quick means to changing the culture of an organisation. However this is an important part of instituting change through the content maturity model. Culture can be defined as a common belief: a set of values or attitudes. It can also be seen as a set of rituals and the means by which things get done.

To start the assessment we need to analyse the attitudes of people receiving new information:

- Do they immediately interpret it differently to how it is intended?
- Do they believe it?
- Do they ask further questions?
- Does the information seem incorrect to them and do they ask for qualification?

Having assessed their responses we should determine the behaviours to be addressed. A number of concerns may be relevant here:

- That their attitudes and beliefs seem to be based on misinterpretations.
- That they are in the wrong place, time and competency.
- That they have insufficient competitive understanding or motivation.
- That they have insufficient time to manage and work with information.

Let us look at each of these areas.

Changing attitudes and beliefs

Culture is made of two key components: attitudes and beliefs. Attitudes are learnt through the experience of using information. Belief is the result of information accumulating over time. To address attitudes we must train people in new tools and collaborative methods to make storing and finding information a better experience than in the past. To address belief we must assess the belief systems and their sources and correct them. We can do this by having open access to all the information. People can be rewarded for joining in the self-assessment and peer review process in order to improve the information sources.

When carrying out information culture change, 90 per cent of people will be persuaded by good corporate information campaigns but others will still be entrenched in their old belief systems. To address this the organisation should consider individual consultation or involvement in the culture change programme.

There are a number of methods to assess beliefs and attitudes:

- Run quality audits to see the difference between what is wished for and what is delivered, by comparing the perspectives of people in different parts of the organisation. This may expose conflicting goals.
- Provide a means by which knowledge can be shared so that people have less need to hold onto it.
- Reward involvement by considering all opinions and inputs, such as by brainstorming techniques where ideas are all equally acceptable and none is discarded out of hand.
- Publicise the success of mentors and their processes throughout the business. No-one wants to be a machine following a re-engineering process chart or a process queue. Let examples be taken from people, not objects, as people work better through personal recommendations.
- Regularly build, change and mix teams, allocating time to discussions about internal processes. Take on board improvements and suggestions and deliver on them.

- Rewards should be facilitated frequently and periodically rather than annually. Try to reward teams, not individuals, to build the sense of the collective organisation.

- Spread good knowledge sharers and mentors around the organisation and in teams. Let them lead by example and encourage the adding of ideas to the conceptual pool.

Organisational structure

Culture is inextricably linked to organisational structure. Roles and responsibilities need to be correctly balanced and assessed on the basis of experience, competency and influence.

Information sources, destinations, stakeholders and audiences are numerous. The Wikipedia definition of information management indicates that it comes in many forms: electronic, physical, ephemeral and spoken ones, and memories and perceptions. When an organisation becomes larger as more people start working together, the management and co-ordination of all the channels of information through its people or systems naturally become geometrically more complex.

In larger organisations it is important to understand why hierarchies are in place, to ensure the timely dissemination of information. To have three people working together, there need to be three communication channel streams. For 20 people to work together 190 channels of communication need to be maintained: hence the need to work in small teams or departments.

An army assigning orders to move in battle does so very effectively: its hierarchy is optimised to reduce the number of channels required. When an organisation is too hierarchical, information often suffers from elaboration or censorship as it passes through the tiers. The flat organisation was born and to remedy this problem through email: the great enabler of communication. Everybody could use email to communicate to anyone, no matter how senior they were. In such an organisation it is hard to determine who leads and makes decisions. However ECM enables flat structures to operate, and information to be accessible to all stakeholders uniformly, or at an appropriate level of detail.

Competitive motivation

Lack of internal competition in an organisation can lead to complacency. There are ways of keeping competition even and well-mannered within the organisation.

First, try to adopt parallel approaches to performing a task. The team which succeeds will teach the other what went right and what it could have done better. Offer simple awards at ceremony nights for the teams which do well. Try to recognise that every team has done something well. Second, make sure that benchmarks are not simply a means to measure whether we should be outsourcing an operation or not. Try to get the benchmarking firm to provide feedback and advice on best practice so that some value comes from the exercise.

Partitioning time

As has already been suggested, everybody should adopt a balance of three key tasks in the working day, week or year:

- training or learning;
- practice or doing something;
- teaching or reviewing.

All projects should have budgets allocated at 20 per cent for learning, 70 per cent for practice and 10 per cent for teaching.

SUMMARY

Information sharing should be at all levels and endemic. Top executives must be shown how to participate in the information management process as much as new employees.

People may not talk glowingly or eloquently of their work, because they may not feel particularly special in comparison to their colleagues. Train and encourage all employees to take their ideas outside: to blogs and to conferences and society meetings. There they can communicate effectively, share their thoughts and, by doing so, promote the organisation.

Here are a number of ideas for making an organisation a knowledge and information-sharing one:

- Make recruitment a test of the ability to share knowledge using games.
- Make the human resources (HR) department a trusted department where all conversations are confidential and an ethical approach to managing people's worries is strictly complied. Hence rumours should always be quashed and stakeholders should not feel that they are putting their jobs or careers on the line by airing grievances or issues. If HR cannot be trusted then no other part of the organisation can. HR drives the ethics movement in the organisation.
- Make any positive behaviour a positive component in an employee's record. If the employee agrees make it public, being clear why the award was given.
- Adopt mentoring as a means of achieving long-term organisational commitment.
- Keep internal and external communities active, ensuring that measurable KPIs on their use are reported upon.

9 TRANSFORMATION

Never tell people how to do things. Tell them what to do and they will surprise you with their ingenuity
General George S. Patton

Transformation is defined as a human-centric, multi-stage, iterative process which aims to create sustainable changes in behaviour in complex systems, organisations and their people. An earlier chapter on the content maturity model defined the goals for organisation at various stages of maturity. Transformation design is a fundamental constituent in the model and describes the process by which an organisation moves between stages.

The aim of transformation in the content maturity process is to deliver improvements to each of the dimensions – people, systems and processes – so that they are aligned at a particular stage. When delivering transformation it is necessary to carry out the improvements in a specific order if they are to be effective: first systems, followed by processes and then people.

The dimensions should be aligned to a particular stage because there is wasted effort throughout an organisation if its resources are not working effectively together. For example dimension alignment allows a demographic of people skills and culture to be correctly mapped. New employees who have emerging experience of social and internet tools are motivated in an organisation which is embracing new techniques as they can establish the tools at an enterprise level. However current employees may need to be trained in the use of tools or given more time to acquaint themselves with the facets of collaborative technologies.

There are several steps to take when establishing the process of transformation:

(a) Build a content organisation framework through automated methods or interviews.

(b) Create a content and information strategy.

(c) Plan.

ORGANISATIONS' CONTENT AND EXCHANGE FRAMEWORKS

An organisation's content and exchange framework maps activities and the value they add as a means to measure the contribution of knowledge workers. It places people into the following categories:

- Subject matter experts (SMEs), who perform analysis and consultation and give advice. They bridge the gap between numerical and experiential analysis and decision making by adopting various levels and methods of communication.

- Project management officers (PMOs), who capture, organise and report on project processes. They provide various levels of communication from temporal and risk analysis of the planning process.

- Research librarians, who establish sources and references and carry out due diligence on information sources. They organise and provide access to information to support the content management process, ensuring that newly acquired knowledge and references are correctly catalogued.

- Collaborative networkers, who communicate through different methods and drive interest and specialist groups by sharing, preserving and moving information across the organisation and its stakeholders.

- Educators, who interpret strategy and policy in content management and ensure that information persists and reaches all parts of the organisation.

- Product technical managers, who support the content distributed as products and services.

There are tools which automatically build the network of influence by analysing the email traffic within an organisation. These can measure the following:

- the spread of communication and the extent of collaborative networking;
- the degree to which information interaction is passive;
- the depth of interaction achieved in engagement to provide support;
- the extent to which people drive the organisation by initiating conversations;
- the degree to which responses copied from earlier correspondence reflect the constructive checks and added value expected.

Where no automated tools are available, information will need to be collected over a suitable period. In a small, fully operational organisation, this might be a week to a month. In large organisations working to financial periods, it might be best to have one to three months of communication analysis.

CREATE A CONTENT AND INFORMATION STRATEGY

An analysis will still be needed for the output of automated organisational network tools in order to qualify and confirm the results through interview. The analysis can be delivered as an information strategy and planned in two phases.The first is to assess the content maturity using the three dimensions, noting the effects of people, systems and processes and identifying areas for change. The second is to assess the current organisation: how it manages content; its current number of incoming documents and electronic messages; its processes for content storage, management and authentication; and its mechanisms for generating new content and assessing its value, if any.

The analysis will need to be communicated, shared and discussed. Conclusions and recommendations should then be derived to develop the content and information strategy.

TRANSFORMATION PLANNING TO AVOID ORGANISATIONAL STRESS

To deliver the content and information strategy a plan will need to be drawn up. Without a plan the transformation would be ill-formed and chaotic.

Organisations which work under duress are rarely efficient. If its approach is not planned then the organisation is at risk of creating fire-sale solutions: quick-fix maintenance resolutions which can quickly unravel and add further complexity to its technology architecture.

When organisations are under stress or forced to work at a quicker rate than their established pace the result can be that important aspects of governance and authority are circumnavigated. Business-at-risk assessments go overlooked and systems break down.

No organisation should sustain long-term stress. There is a risk of an increased attrition rate, reduced retention of key staff, an imbalance of back-office to front-office staff, and transaction and throughput bottlenecks. Such incidents have been triggered, for example, by outsourcing or support transfer being inappropriately resourced.

Managing around points of stress can be a serious drain on the energy and progress of an organisation. Moving up the stages in the content maturity model is a good way to overcome the stress, but doing so while under strain may create more problems. To avoid this, always plan to mitigate the risk of these stresses by moving before they become issues.

BRINGING DIMENSIONS INTO ALIGNMENT

The aim when working with the content maturity model is to bring all the dimensions into alignment at a stage where the organisation is effective. Typically an organisation aims for the enterprise stage as the first milestone in its plan for content maturity, and as part of a long-term information management strategy. The key to reducing stress in the organisation is not necessarily to improve one dimension over another, it is to reduce the differences between or dominance in specific dimensions.

Reducing differences in the people dimension
The content maturity model requires that the organisation's people are well trained, to enable progress through the stages. A tuned organisation will have a high level of expectation from the people involved with and controlling its systems.

Figure 9.1 People dimension differences

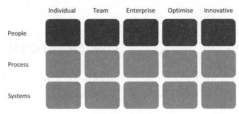

There may be a surfeit of skilled personnel inside an organisation. The challenge will be to ensure that it can promote their involvement, manage their contribution and reward them effectively.

An organisation's knowledge must be greater than the sum of its people's knowledge. For people to engage in a system they must trust that it will accept and distribute contributions transparently, and without barriers to access.

Consider the functional boundary between the capabilities of ECM and the people it serves. There are clear roles which can be enhanced through ECM: capturing and promoting ideas through forums for example. However there are specific facets of management which should always retain a human element: listening, mentoring or reflecting, giving direction and motivating.

Figure 9.2 ECM and people functional boundaries

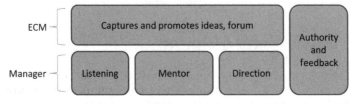

To be used a system must support the capturing, progression, creativity and communication of ideas. It must do everything a good manager would to build cohesion after acquisition and assure that common goals are sought.

Weaknesses in the people dimension can be put down to one or more of the following:

- not addressing the differences in people and culture emanating from staff reluctance to adopt change or conformity;

- not addressing the compensation and reward system to match the expectations of the employees and the true value added by its people;

- not addressing the imbalances in the organisation, whether too top- or bottom-heavy;

- not addressing the fact that power and responsibility are incorrectly distributed.

By assessing the above weaknesses and correcting them the organisation will reduce the differences in its people dimension.

Reducing differences in the process dimension

When the organisation is overtly process-centric, it may become bound by its complete and definitive definition, which will be difficult and exhausting to maintain. Processes may be defined and implemented in such detail that the organisation may spend more than 10 per cent of its time and effort in just manipulating and managing the process definition. The process of making and agreeing changes is laborious. As the definition becomes the preserve of a few in the organisation, its people tend to avoid changing the process in the formalised way by simply accepting the process as it stands or making changes or adjustments to it without reporting them.

Figure 9.3 Process dimension differences

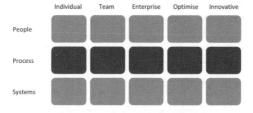

Where process definition is immature and inconsistent, ECM can manage the co-ordination of quality, information and accessibility. It will make the process of creating a definition a clear and collaborative one from the start.

In order to balance the opposing extremes of a dominant or an immature process definition system, a web-delivered process management system should be made available to all. This means that changes can be managed centrally and transparently.

Consider the functional boundary between the capabilities of ECM and the processes within the organisation. ECM is proficient in managing mundane version control, filing and distribution. However it does not extend to understanding inherent meaning in process representation by reflecting on critical paths and optimisation. There are other tools which excel at managing process representation. Where process maps are interpreted using XML-like structures, automated systems can be controlled or filing hierarchies used.

Figure 9.4 ECM and process functional boundaries

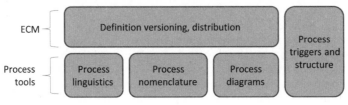

Specialised tools may be needed to manage organisational and hierarchical descriptions of processes. These tools manage the universal non-specialised nomenclature and iconography of process definition beyond the scope of ECM, so that they are accepted by everybody in the organisation.

Reducing differences in the systems dimension

When the systems dimension lags behind the other dimensions, the technology and tools to enable efficient use and delivery of content are not in place.

Figure 9.5 System dimension differences

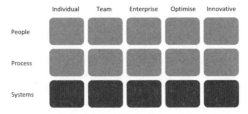

At any of the maturity stages there will be applications which generate data. Without co-ordination, categorisation or simplification the data produced will create problems beyond the intended reports on which they are based.

Consider the functional boundary between the capabilities of ECM and the systems with which it works. Clear roles can be defined through ECM content governance to ensure that there is no duplication of effort or control, although there are common components in search and security which are shared between infrastructure systems and ECM systems.

Figure 9.6 ECM and systems functional boundaries

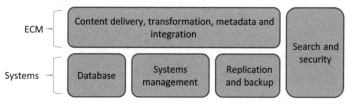

ECM is particularly good at working logically with information. However as platform technologies change rapidly ECM development has recognised that some infrastructural components are readily optimised, and should be accepted. ECM is a fine balance between inventing new mechanisms and technologies and using incumbent technologies.

The right expectations must be set for the benefits of technology. Organisations need to ensure that their technology delivers realistic improvements. They need to sustain a reputation for delivery: this can be tarnished by the often complex adoption and delivery of ECM components.

A re-scoping of the business case for such a technology implementation will reduce the expectations for each phase of delivery. Thus the delivery reputation of the IT part of the organisation is retained or even enhanced.

When the systems dimension is far superior to the other dimensions at a maturity stage, it is likely that over-capacity is eroding the ECM benefits to the business. The applications need to be tuned to the business. IT must not be seen to drive the business or deliver applications which are not needed or adaptable. A business requirements catalogue, and an architecture and capability matrix, are essential tools for maintaining a level of control and perspective.

TRANSITIONING THROUGH STAGES

There are a number of guidelines and activities for ensuring smooth transition between stages. Evolution through the stages should be carried out step by step rather than by leaping across stages. It is good programme and project practice to carry out transformation in measured steps, so as to avoid corporate shock from leaping too quickly or too far.

An example of corporate shock during transformation took place during the internet bubble. New organisations were encouraged to become global enterprises at a pace which their natural infrastructure, process and people could not manage. Their business financial plans were built on acquiring and retaining a large number of customers with simple low-cost products or advertising revenues. All of these failed to materialise.

Moving to the team stage

When moving to the team stage a number of activities must be carried out. These are:

Figure 9.7 Moving to the team stage

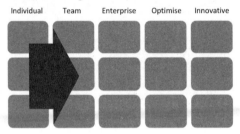

- developing the ECM infrastructure to support teamwork, but with an eye to working globally through the use of web technologies;

- starting to move data by consolidating information and content repositories, using a set of methods which could become the basis for migration at future stages;

- recognising knowledge workers and managing the analysis of information by creating roles for analysing content and categorising it. This involves finding out and adopting best practices from the industry and competitors;

- communicating the content maturity model to stakeholders, especially those who have a vested interest in the growth and maintenance of their information repositories;

- ensuring that, as in all significant enterprise projects, executive sponsorship from the highest levels is forthcoming.

Migration is not an exact science but good practice leads to the establishment of a master data management system or structure to ensure migration can be continuous. Content management requires continuous consolidation, migration and transformation. As organisations join with or acquire new organisations, they also acquire information system assets, not just the capital and human ones.

In the initial stages there should be a bridgehead governance group with a handful of people who can assess information assets, analyse reporting requirements, identify and catalogue source data locations, create records management policies and construct information metrics. These operational units can be initiated by the use of specialist ECM consultancy services which can quickly set up all the content assessment and delivery frameworks. The initiation service should train, and hand over the governance role to, the people within the organisation. Periodic audits should take place to ensure the governance operation is cost-effective and provides continuous benefits.

Governance groups must also have the authority to ensure contributions are made by managers or those who have committed to the ECM transformation.

Moving from the team to the enterprise stage

Unless the organisation is a single team, the team stage should rarely be a final goal.

Figure 9.8 Moving to the enterprise stage

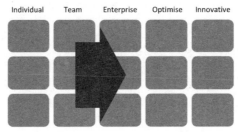

Small organisations that have grown organically may have temporarily built capacity to initiate the foundations. However they see the advantages of consolidated repositories and providing a central governance structure which continues to bind teams together.

There are further activities at this transition:

- make the data and content into a single organisational repository having merged and consolidated teams data

- build central co-ordinating teams or centres of excellence which can maintain architecture, governance, data and content standards at enterprise level
- focus on communication across the organisation, making it regular and frequent
- ensure that the delivery mechanism for content is universal and straightforward to secure
- align reporting tools to engage in organisational-wide perspectives, co-opting enterprise-level metrics
- practice continuous improvement and integration

The metrics used for enterprise-level reporting for content should include:

- growth in content requested and supplied over financial periods, including revenues directly or indirectly attributed to that content
- comparative content analysis and market penetration against competitors and how much content is supplied
- customer satisfaction surveys captured by content and web delivery systems in terms of length of stay and commitment to retain subscriptions
- process efficiencies captured as part of the process analytics in the ECM suite
- skill self-assessment matrices and how they improve over time

Moving from the enterprise to the optimise stage

Once the enterprise has been established, the organisation is ideally placed to start the journey to the optimise stage. This incorporates a number of tasks:

Figure 9.9 Moving to the optimise stage

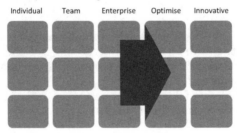

- establishing market metrics so that the organisation can be tuned to the market and not to its own internal market view;
- adopting a continuous process improvement practice, like Six Sigma, to ensure that all processes remain tuned;
- building the learning and teaching roles into all people's roles so that systems can enable continuous learning and the dissemination of knowledge;
- enlarging the business intelligence model to include metrics relevant to all external stakeholders, partners, suppliers and customers;
- re-engineering the incentive scheme to ensure that co-operation and collaboration are rewarded and include all the people in the business, not just the sales and partner programmes;
- ensuring that all managers co-ordinate their efforts at an organisational level.

Organisations at the enterprise stage will have adopted unstructured information in many forms. The metrics more suited to these organisations might be:

- managing brands and information assets which relate to the cost of ownership. Sales growth should be aligned not just to the product, but to all aspects of the product, including its support and marketing;
- monitoring how many information and data assets are turned over or thrown away and making that a measure of how effectively the process maintains the integrity of the knowledge system;
- monitoring the usage levels of key information services, such as search and retrieval, to see that they remain efficient. The organisation should also measure the amount of time used by each a particular role in these processes;
- monitoring any processes or exceptions which are rarely used, and looking for skews in the business to ensure there is no avoidance practice;
- measuring the cost of acquisition and storage of core information sources and the sales revenue from delivered information and content;
- measuring the cost of the knowledge worker process, to ensure contributions are as effective as required using the new incentive models;
- measuring the time to market for a piece of content.

Moving from optimise to innovative stages

The tasks for this move are a subtle extension those from the previous transition. We should encourage diversity by employing a greater variety of people who can question and think in unusual ways. This will allow the organisation to adopt discontinuous association techniques to innovate.

Figure 9.10 Moving to the innovative stage

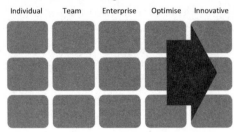

Architects should build an infrastructure which can tap into information that passes through it without necessarily taking ownership. By sampling specific data sets the organisation becomes more efficient. This is akin to search engine robots not needing to store all the information, but simply the links to it.

Organisations' sources of information should be expanded. The tapping of information through web services should be automated and feeds instantiated to maintain accuracy and relevance.

At the innovative stage the opportunity is to become an experimental, research-led organisation rather than a manufacturing one. For example in Cuba the medical research facilities are world-renowned, creating excellent long-term revenues from vaccines. Research is what continues to makes pharmaceutical companies profitable in spite of the arduous clinical proof required.

As in most organisations which plan well, a corporate risk mitigation portfolio should be maintained. This ensures that continuous change does not destabilise the organisation.

In creating ECM metrics the following should be considered:

- continuously valuing the documents in the repository according to their direct correlation to the delivered content used in services and products;
- measuring the value of content storage and delivery partnerships to product development, and assessing them for continuation on a 12–24 month basis;
- attributing the asset value of the portfolio of high-yielding sources and content relevant to delivered services;
- retaining close control of intellectual property, especially patents and relationship records, as these are important organisational assets;
- determining the proportion of documents in creative and collaborative states, their time in these states, and whether they are used as reference documents used or archive ones.

SUMMARY

In this chapter we have walked through the tasks required to navigate the dimensions of the content maturity model. It is particularly important to understand what ECM can and cannot do. We have seen where ECM's functional boundaries lie for people, processes and systems. We have introduced good governance practice at early stages based on master data management, Six Sigma and the temporary use of experts to establish foundations quickly and train the organisation to move through the maturity stages.

10 COMPLIANCE AND GOVERNANCE FRAMEWORK

Those grateful acts, those thousand decencies, that daily flow from all her words and actions, mixed with love and sweet compliance, which declare unfeigned union of mind, or in us both one soul
John Milton

This chapter describes the building of a governance and compliance framework with ECM. A robust and future-proof framework should be:

- pervasive and available wherever required;
- integrated seamlessly into current process practices;
- universally applicable to the enterprise;
- integrated into current systems to a significant extent;
- modular and capable of expansion.

The framework should define who is responsible for what and how decisions concerning information are made and communicated. The business characteristics are examined more fully in the business guide. In the meantime let us look at the systems characteristics.

Figure 10.1, for example, provides an overview of the Sarbanes Oxley compliance framework and the drivers for mechanisms to manage it. The annotation can be found in www.southbeachinc.com. Note that there are two key control mechanisms in compliance: process management and information governance.

There are a number of ECM framework policies which must be formulated when reviewing the compliance framework:

- content destruction policies;
- enterprise metrics;
- security;
- trust and privacy policies;
- data governance;
- records management.

Figure 10.1 Sarbanes Oxley compliance framework, overtly simplified

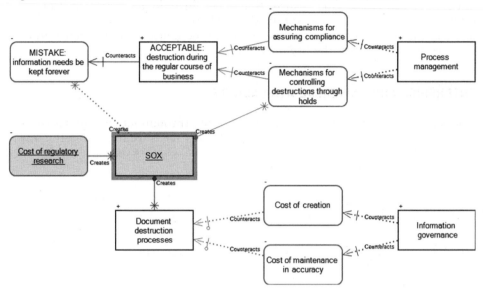

TRUST AND PRIVACY POLICIES

As part of the organisation's responsibility to assure stakeholders of the accuracy and consistency of information held, trust and privacy policies need to be drawn up. Any governance framework should have the tools to improve the quality of data by analysis and correction across the organisation. Services which fall into this category should:

- reduce duplication by defining the master data sources;
- detect anomalies and inconsistencies on live data as it emerges rather than periodically;
- define and retain standards and adopt industry and organisational taxonomies;
- define levels of access for sources.

DESTRUCTION POLICIES

There may be a mistaken belief that Sarbanes Oxley compliance means that information must be kept forever. Destruction of records during the regular course of business is perfectly acceptable. This simple statement is tempered by the need to provide a legal holds process so that record destruction is safe during imminent investigations or audit actions.

The process for destruction of records must be documented and maintained and relate to a well documented, universally acceptable and accessible set of business processes. This ensures that these business process definitions relate to living documents or applications. There are tools which provide a web delivery platform for process maps which can be understood, amended and checked by all levels of the organisation.

ENTERPRISE AND UNIVERSAL AVAILABILITY

It is important that compliance solutions apply throughout the enterprise. Whether the enterprise is small or large, the key measure for understanding whether enterprise applies to the organisation is whether any of the following are important in its running:

- growth: the enterprise will be growing rapidly so the solution must be scalable;
- durability: the enterprise will be working 24/7 so the solution must be robust, supporting disaster recovery configurations and failover;
- global operations: the enterprise works across countries and languages, so must have the capability to work across all these variations in a logical and organised manner.

Only companies which have these characteristics should really consider these availability aims viable.

The art of good architecture is to understand when and when not to use technology. Drawing the demarcation in a business between non-technical and technical capabilities and how they meet, complement and interact – without a gap appearing in the business capability – is an important aspect of being an architect.

There are some key questions to ask at this juncture:

- Have the standards and regulations which relate to the organisation been identified and catalogued?
- Is each one understood and is its impact measured, together with the penalties for non-compliance with these standards on business processes?
- Is there insurance to cover this?
- Do third-party contracts include compliance objectives and clauses for non-compliance?
- Are the staff trained to understand the liabilities of non-compliance?

SECURITY

As more than a third of staff with administration rights to information systems admit to snooping, having local access to systems is often not a good thing. The general rule is: the fewer administrators the better.

With almost 75 per cent of administrators saying they could bypass controls to protect data, this becomes a deeper concern. Administrators have admitted that they would take information with them if they were fired, although what they could do with it is usually of little consequence. There may be people who would use such information but normally such people are in a different sphere of influence: the truth is administrators and businessmen rarely mix.

Whether middlemen in camel hair coats could facilitate these two groups mixing is another matter. The significance of information is normally only personally political within the organisation it comes from, or to well organised criminal gangs who would extort money from access to secret or sensitive information. The aim for security is to ensure that the organisation does not walk anywhere near these categories.

Often the case for information is based on a character: that of the perpetrator. Usually this is because newspapers are keen to pin the misdemeanour on a person, and traditionally corporations rarely have high-profile or public people.

The following types of information, although not exhaustive, illustrate the types of information at risk:

- undisclosed financial reports;
- merger and acquisition plans;
- R&D plans;
- CEO passwords;
- HR information;
- redundancy lists;
- customer databases.

DATA GOVERNANCE

An ECM Strategy should be supported by a framework or blueprint on which all the ECM services are described. The aim of the framework is to represent the processes of capture, integration and delivery of information whilst also identifying points of transformation at which there are risks to accuracy, inconsistency and delay. The first and fundamental component of a framework is to define and manage data governance and the records management scheme.

Data governance is fundamental to the maintenance of an ECM system. As part of the technical planning and implementation process, the project team must be set up to define the data to be controlled by the system.

There are a number of specialist applications of data which need to be controlled:

- content data type and the storage of complex data;
- attributes, tags and indexes;

- XML and encapsulation;
- taxonomies.

Content data type

Unstructured data – that which could not be fitted within the relational model with standard text, numeric and date formats – are stored separately. They are managed by storing the binary data in a large file, separate from the database record file, which contains many other blocks of data (i.e. BLOBs). The majority of binary objects are stored at the beginning of block margins in the file – usually aligned to the block size, for example 8012 bytes – so that only the block number needs to be stored in the relational table.

Relational systems concentrate their functionality around text, numeric and date functions to get the best performance out of a structured database. ECM systems extended the complex structure with control over the BLOB or external file. Some were created as plug-ins or were developed with new engines to extend the SQL locking mechanisms to work with these new extensible data types.

An example of these is the spatial data type. Spatial data represents multi-dimensional shapes in space by collecting the sets of vectors or lines which make up their shapes. Specialist functions were then developed around determining the area in a two-dimensional layer or volume bound by the spatial data. Hence it was straightforward to have a query which enabled the user to determine the smallest shape, intersections with other shapes, the shape's centre, the shape with the least number of sides (vectors or nodes) or the nearest shape to a point.

In ECM the data are just as complex and compelling in terms of functions which could be useful. Specialist functions are used throughout: finding a word in a block of text while including its stemmed variant is a useful feature, for example.

Attributes, tags and indexes

When developing attributes or indexes due consideration should be given to their maintenance. Fewer attributes will mean lower costs in maintenance. This is balanced with the need to improve granularity of search. What you lose in granularity of indexes you gain in maintenance.

The collecting of document attributes, tags and indexes in a catalogue is just as important as the document itself. These are important intellectual facets which will also need to be maintained.

A balance must be struck between capturing complex and detailed tags, maintaining them, and continually assessing the value of the original document for retention. This is shown in Figure 10.2.

Figure 10.2 Balancing attribute assignment

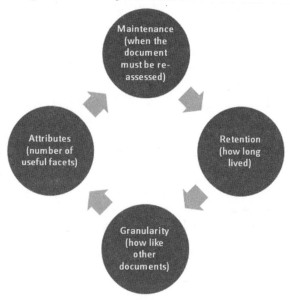

There is a dichotomy between maintaining a free set of attributes which represents a complex content object and the essence of maintaining a structure or taxonomy which allows the document to be retrieved. Therefore attributes should be kept logically separate: logical and numeric identifiers and organisational data – e.g. business divisions – should be separated from the taxonomy of categories which relates to the industry semantics and is closely aligned to the language of the organisation.

XML and encapsulation

The use of XML as a universal container and descriptive envelope has a fundamental impact on ECM. XML has enabled documents to be enveloped into a multifaceted object which is transparent and human-readable so that it can be inspected for attached attributes but also re-rendered into another document where necessary.

This has provided system designers with the components for encapsulation of the attributes together with the essential contents of the original document. Documents can now contain universal references to other documents and therefore also the collection of the document record. More important the references inside the XML are to virtual and generic references so that objects can be placed in different places for placement in storage.

There is an argument for encapsulating the attributes of the document by extending the document envelope to contain extensible attributes provided by the business. The most complex document types, such as Word and PDF, have internal structures which allow internal properties to be maintained. When this happens you only need to maintain the document, not the indexes or attributes which surround it. However the disadvantage of this approach is that a document necessarily does not maintain an audit of all changes and could be edited out of conformance to the need to maintain the original copy as it is.

The balance of function to accuracy should be carefully measured on whether the content itself falls into an auditable content type. For example transactions are simple structured types and naturally require support for audit. Only highly specific pieces of content fall into this class for audit. Maintaining different classes of content therefore allows different basic records management rules to be used at the most appropriate cost.

Taxonomy

A taxonomy describes the organisation's specialist and industry nomenclature in a structured manner, very much like a thesaurus. All documents within it are then categorised against that taxonomy. This makes finding them easier and more straightforward because the meanings of all indexed documents will be consistent.

If taxonomies are to be effective they must closely mirror the understanding, nomenclature and vocabulary of an organisation. ECM uses taxonomies so that content storage can be managed and classified clearly, universally and transparently.

Organisations rarely adopt a universal business dictionary or thesaurus because they are different and the ways they work with content can be extraordinarily diverse. A taxonomy would need to define a number of ways in which an organisation can see its documents:

- by document type, e.g. medical files, video sequences or crime reports;
- by relevance to the business process or purpose, e.g. sales, support or customer contacts;
- by the products and services they relate to, e.g. washing machines or consulting assignments;
- by geographic regions, e.g. Europe, Paris, Benelux or wheat-belt states• by industry sectors, e.g. finance-insurance, FMCG or government health;
- by audiences e.g. customers, clients or partners;
- by organisational criteria, e.g. human resources, legal or engineering;
- by topics, e.g. strategy, recovery or customer choices.

Taxonomies are created quickly through the use of an available business taxonomy, industry sector or historic source already in use within the organisation. Once created they are improved and tuned as the ECM system ingests more documents. A taxonomy should always reflect what the organisation is doing now.

Back-scanning is the process by which the current set of documents and content is scanned into the ECM system. This is the ideal time to test the emerging taxonomy. It is also a time to ensure that what is scanned is of direct value within the early stages of the systems evolution. If documents of no value to the current organisational processes are scanned then they should be discarded.

Outsourcing documents for back-scanning may be a false economy. Having staff adopt the indexing process as soon as practicable is an important part of gaining acceptance for the ECM repository as well as ensuring that it is fit for purpose.

Considerable effort is still required to ensure the taxonomy does not lead down false alleys or to an inappropriate vocabulary. Many organisations fail in their ECM indexing processes from the start because these are not optimised for everyday use, are arduous to maintain and are impossible to navigate. Key staff should review the taxonomy regularly and ensure the number and depth of terms are useful.

Content systems should be able to reduce the 'tag' cloud, purge documents or reassign documents to other, more appropriate, classes. Document classes ensure that the index terms or tags are focused within the document class, rather than covering a number of unrelated document classes. Procedures should be in place to manage the cleansing of data, and maintain the reference taxonomy and the overall catalogue.

There are a number of basic taxonomic rules:

- People's and organisation names or proper nouns should be avoided wherever appropriate, because these will change and the content will become quickly out of date or unsearchable.

- Topics should be as generic and as simple as possible.

- Taxonomies should be inclusive, not exhaustive.

- Industry and government standards should be incorporated wherever available.

- Enterprise product names and lines of business should be included.

The document aims, strengths and conclusions are often more important than the subject matter. Good content reuse allows the transferral of ideas to new contexts.

RECORDS MANAGEMENT

There are several considerations in a records management strategy:

- There will be a need to identify all information repositories, whether physical or electronic, from filing cabinet folders to server databases.

- All storage media on which information is stored must be identified, whether in paper or disk format.

- Media must be tracked through the repositories from their creation to their destruction, so it will be known where a piece of information is at any time.

- Instances of information considered fundamental to the business cycle must be captured, i.e. web pages on the sale of goods, copies of manuals which go out with products etc.

We can encapsulate the essence of understanding the risk and reach of records management through Figure 10.3 (the notation for this diagram can be found through www.southbeachinc.com).

Figure 10.3 Records management control risks

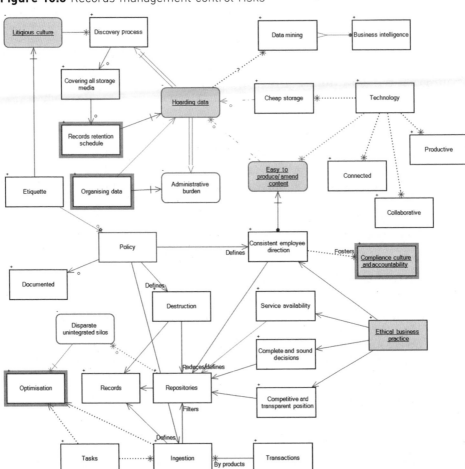

The diagram emphasises the driving issues and risks with records management, which are:

- that even though we may start with an intention of organising information and having a records retention policy, it is hard to manage this with a background of litigious corporate culture. It is also hard to balance it with the lackadaisical culture of hoarding data, and easy storage, which IT departments are so willing to serve the business by;

- that ethical business practice must be endemic and policies easily understood and maintained;

- that disparate un-integrated silos will break down and make the optimisation of repositories and their controls harder;

- The false or unproven hope that the art of business intelligence using data mining technology may make hoarding a useful behaviour.

There is a mission in records management that:

- the right data can be quickly and effectively retrieved from the organisation's systems;

- the right information at the right time will enable the organisation to make the right decisions;

- clear objectives can be set so that the correct versions of information, which make sense for business continuity, are stored.

Once all of these have been catalogued and tracked the cost of maintenance, both in environmental and technology terms, can be assessed. As a result the information management operation can be optimised.

The decision to store everything is not necessarily a wise one for the majority of organisations. This is especially the case when litigious citizens or organisations feel affected by damage due to information which an organisation may hold or create. It ensures that the business which creates information, either through reports or emails, must be well versed in what it retains, in terms of proving its value add, or discards as out-of-date information.

SUMMARY

The key to managing records, then, is focusing on processes: service availability, transparent reporting and decision processes. After over 20 years of process management, the easy and universal adoption of process management tools in the same way as a word processor is still a long way off.

In establishing a framework for compliance, policies for destruction, measurement, security and trust need to be formulated. An organisation needs to understand which facets of enterprise drive it: growth, criticality or global presence. Once this is understood the compliance framework can be appropriately structured.

An information strategy must have at least data governance and records management defined.

11 BUSINESS AND PROGRAMME DELIVERY

It is delivery that makes the orator's success
Johann Wolfgang von Goethe

In this chapter we describe how to follow through with the business case implementation, deploy a programme and meet the challenges of delivery.

BUILDING THE BUSINESS CASE

The characteristics of a successful business case are that it must:

- persuade a variety of audiences through an effective summary;
- understand the competitive landscape;
- make financial sense;
- document all the assumptions clearly;
- be tightly scoped;
- be aligned to strategic goals.

We will take each of these areas of the business case and review what makes these areas important.

Effective executive summary

To persuade a variety of audiences there should be a short, concise executive summary. This is likely to be the only thing which people will read and should be written first. It sets the goal for the business case and should be revisited regularly throughout its construction.

The business case summary should encapsulate the rationale for the project in simple terms. It should be drafted, revisited with sponsors and redrafted on a regular basis.

It should do this in a picture, ensuring scope is well mapped out, and use white space, short paragraphs, bullet points and at least a simple diagram. Executives need to be convinced within the first three minutes of reading the summary.

Complete market analysis

The ECM business case must show an understanding of the organisation, its customers' needs and the size, scope and reach of its operations. The business case must consider the market in which the organisation operates and how it may change, including the potential for new competitors through innovation, acquisitions and distributions. The analysis should cover the life of the project or programme and, wherever possible, use independent research studies.

Sound financial case

The organisation must be in a position to meet the demands of the business case. The business case should identify whether there is a need for training, replacing and supplementing skills with expertise or specialist management on a temporary or permanent basis. The cost of filling in this skill or training gap must be included.

To make business sense the financial projections should be realistic. For example a successful business case in financial services will need to show payback in the first year. Implementation periods in ECM may typically take more than one year, so it is essential to gain incremental value early on.

In some markets content may be a competitive differentiator and market ground may be lost if a project does not go ahead. All business cases should consider the likely position of an organisation if it does nothing.

Collate assumptions

At the beginning of the process all the assumptions should be documented. This allows the business case to be reassessed and tuned as it develops, or when further significant information comes to light. The assumptions must be recorded accurately and reviewed throughout the project. The criteria by which the assumptions change should also be recorded.

One person should be in charge of collating assumptions so that, if changes or checks to assumptions occur, their context and weighted effect can be assessed consistently. The assumptions should be grouped and prioritised by high-level assumptions to keep the number manageable, and to ensure that those used to drive the business case are retained.

Manage scope

Scope is an important part of developing a business case. The number of variables in a business case can increase the time and cost burden of providing a persuasive and justifiable case.

For example there might be three basic dimensions to a business case:

- potential growth (negative, static or positive);
- operational market (national, European or global);
- product line (widget A, B or C).

The scenarios which are developed and presented in the business case need to present a set of scenarios which are realistic within these three dimensions. Just presenting the three dimensions with the above combinations could produce 27 different scenarios. All of these need to be catered for but only a handful need be considered. In this case global growth is unlikely to be predictable, and some widgets may actually not be marketable for wider distribution beyond certain borders. Hence there are only likely to be four key combinations which are useful.

If a director shown this example asks for another completely new dimension to be considered, for example customer segment, this could make the business case a particularly difficult one to contain and justify.

The person responsible for the arbitration of the business case must ensure that it is consistent, and must govern the scope so that any variation does not skew its overall impact.

Alignment to strategic goals
Strategic goals are often aligned to an information management strategy.

The fundamentals of an information strategy may be described as follows:

- recognition that information is a corporate asset;
- recognition that information must be open and sharable so that corporate knowledge can persist. People need to be coerced and exploited into sharing their knowledge in an open organised manner, so that the corporate body can protect itself when people or parts of it are dispersed;
- recognition that the corporate infrastructure should inherently retain and organise information which is shared so that it is protected from loss but also promoted for reuse or reference.

Information management, often called data quality management strategy, affects all those in an organisation. Everybody becomes accountable in the preservation of the strategy. The organisation's people will need training in the strategy's policies, processes and technologies.

The information management strategy gives rise to an ECM framework in which all services are defined. This has been described in the previous chapter.

PROGRAMME AND PROJECT MANAGEMENT

ECM is corporate long-term strategy which needs to be considered a programme of work involving a number of projects designed to enable and control the organisation's content.

ECM touches most if not every application and system in the organisation. It is best then to align and address portions of the ECM strategy through defined steps and benefits which are self-standing, ensuring that business value is paramount, rather than aim for technical change and simplicity.

In all project endeavours scope is a fundamental parameter. The scope can be organisational, geographic, system-related, applications-related, information-related and timeline-related. Scope creep, as originally brought up earlier in this chapter, should be avoided unless circumstances demand a re-evaluation. It is essential that each project delivers what was promised within small, distinct phases.

There are a number of project management practices which can aid delivery:

- breaking implementation into manageable steps;
- engaging with stakeholders;
- meeting organisations' key strategic objectives;
- managing risk;
- keeping proposal evaluation open;
- senior management ownership;
- maintaining supplier relationships;
- ensuring team integration.

BREAKING IMPLEMENTATION INTO MANAGEABLE STEPS

ECM projects can be classed as either IT- or Business-led projects. When IT-led they tend to be big-bang; when business-led they tend to be incremental.

The number of milestones should be kept to a realistic number. It should be under four for any implementation, with delivery timescales kept very short to ensure that changes do not creep into the implementation.

The project manager and sponsor should be prepared to stop the project if circumstances mean the business benefits are no longer achievable, or no longer represent value for money. Project managers must consider what contingency planning needs to be put in place in case a project is not delivered on time.

Engaging with stakeholders
As ECM's scope is often large it is important to ensure that all stakeholders are engaged. When assigning roles of the customer perspective there must be a sound user-oriented, not technical, rationale for the ECM implementation.

All stakeholders will need to understand and agree baseline requirements. Each will need to be managed to ensure buy-in. They will be measured on a scale so that their resistance to change can be addressed and their key drivers of reward and accountability maintained. Only ever allocate risk to those stakeholders who are best able to manage it. Conflicting priorities must always be resolved before the start of implementation.

All stakeholder viewpoints must be built into the business case. A representation of the current cultural landscape must be described, updated and retained, together with a number of key goals which may be achieved by the implementation. For example staff in Department A will be more proactive as they take more control of and responsibility for the process.

Meeting organisations' key strategic priorities
There is likely to be a lack of synchronicity between the ECM implementation and the organisation's key strategy priorities. The ECM implementation has to be placed in perspective to other projects and, more important, the operational timetable for the organisation. The critical success factors, including the measures of success, need to be agreed with stakeholders and suppliers.

A plan should include provisions for business change, including benefits realisation, as well as the technical implementation.

The implementation timescale needs to be realistic and include consideration for external project and statutory dependencies or clarifications. Consider beforehand which of time, cost, scope and quality is to be sacrificed when problems, risks or conflicts occur.

Keeping proposal evaluation open
Evaluations of proposals need to consider the whole-life value for money, taking account of capital, maintenance and service costs. Ensure you have a balanced evaluation approach which considers financial factors equally with quality and security of delivery, criticality and business drivers.

Managing risk
The ECM project team need to be skilled and experienced with clearly defined roles and responsibilities. Where there is a skill shortfall consider having access to external and accountable expertise.

Identify all the risks and assess their impact and likelihood. Ensure the budget makes the requisite allowances for developing mitigations against high-impact or high-likelihood risks, and that the risk register is agreed and shared with all stakeholders and suppliers.

Ensure there a system by which benefits agreed in the business case can be measured during implementation.

Ensure that bad news reaches senior management so that appropriate action can be correctly sponsored. Make sure that expectations are set so that senior management can prepare methods and mechanisms for agreeing upon options for dealing with conflicts and issues as they arise.

Senior management ownership

ECM projects tend to traverse organisational boundaries. In these cases there needs to be clear governance to maintain alignment with the overall organisational objectives.

Communications between senior managers and considered agreement must be maintained when making organisational commitments and announcements which have delivery implications. Decisions need to be early, decisive, clear and followed to ensure successful delivery.

Senior managers must have the ability, responsibility and authority to ensure changes and benefits are delivered. Always consider refresher training in principles of change to help responsible owners understand their commitment to the project. Motivation driven from the top of the organisation will often need to be seeded by an outside mentor.

Maintaining supplier relationships

Ensure that the suppliers are brought into the project timescale and agree that it is achievable. Reset expectations by removing sales personnel from the process, as they would try to maintain an unrealistic timescale to match the sale. Engage an independent consultant to assure the project business case, timescale and estimates are realistic.

Ensure that assumptions have been clearly recorded by each supplier when they make their proposals, and that sufficient interest from suppliers will be forthcoming.

Ensure that you understand the current strategic state of the industry and therefore supply-side risks. The effects of a supplier buyout or failure can stall a project. As in all supplier engagements, all parties need to know their key roles and responsibilities, with a shared understanding of desired outcomes, key terms and deadlines.

Ensuring team integration

Ensure you understand the implications for your market if you engage in an ECM project. The competitive advantages are often significant, but they depend on whether your industry has the correct number of large organisations and level of substantive generic lethargy to warrant an early and courageous adoption of fundamental technology. Ensure that suppliers are integrated from a perspective of agreeing the objectives. Consider sharing efficiency gains throughout the supply chain.

DELIVERY CHALLENGES

Even with all the good project and programme management practices, there are still challenges in the delivery of ECM:

- managing the classification process;
- controlling the channel of communication;
- managing legacy;
- integrating business compliance;
- reducing the effect of change;
- retaining business policies and requirements;
- valuing documents;
- categorising documents across all the business;
- adopting standardisation;
- focusing on total cost of ownership.

CLASSIFICATION PROCESS

When starting on the road of ECM it is important to catalogue and categorise all the information assets to be contained. Classification can be separated into three areas: business processes, record sets and document types.

Business processes reflect how the organisation is organised, its sub-groups and its teams. They directly indicate the activities and tasks which take place within it. During the process interviews with the organisation's staff, an inventory will emerge of all information holdings, alongside an understanding of the overall goal of the person involved in managing the creation of, or adding value to, that information. It is imperative that the location and form of the asset are identified. There are a number of tools which are relevant to managing the capture of processes.

The record set or series is defined as a group of transaction records. Together these form a corporate transaction. A file plan is then linked to the record set specifying the lowest level of detail using groups of document types, i.e. the media on which the information is stored.

For each record set it is important to:

- determine how the information is created and retained if a failure of systems occurs;
- understand if the information has ephemeral or social value as a historic record which explains the organisation's history;
- determine and agree upon who in the organisation will be the holder of the record, to avoid duplication of responsibility.

Controlling the channel of communication

The format of the information which the organisation is working with, as well as the mechanisms to communicate those formats, will add complexity to the project. Keep the number of communication channels to a handful, delivering them one at a time. For example deliver to one major communication channel at a time depending on the priority of the business: paper, followed by the internet, followed by voice. Test the core delivery mechanism for one knowing that, if the ECM system can deliver core controls to one, it may be extended to others later on.

Legacy management

Legacy systems holding operational data, content management, records management, process management, email, knowledge management and document management must all be considered. Each should be managed separately and specifically for the value it holds.

The documents in these systems are rarely able to follow the standard document lifecycle model. Process management systems are inherently difficult to manage change midstream: the adoption of new processes can create difficulties in current or legacy process queues. Understand the differences between lifecycle models and see that they are unified or simplified to ensure that most valuable documents are incorporated without too much customisation.

Integrating business compliance

It is often good practice to assume that non-technology solutions are often a cost-effective alternative to solving a problem. Not every technological solution is the most appropriate choice. Integration is of no use unless the business process is also addressed and the solution, whether technical or non-technical, used at the most appropriate time.

Reducing the effect of change

The mantra by which enterprise compliance solutions in ECM should be expressed is 'pervasive, not invasive'. Solutions should be available wherever required. Whether it is a technology channel or partner channel there should be mechanisms available to ensure that we can enforce adequate control on all influential systems. It is particularly important to ensure that there is minimal disruption to the business by reducing the amount of change or flux.

Business policies and requirements

There are a handful of key strategic policy guidelines which are typically adopted by an organisation. There should be a single point of access, where all staff can access content without specific systems geared to do so. This should be integrated at the desktop and accessible remotely or through the intranet or internet.

The interface or application should be straightforward and intuitive in finding information – searching across multiple repositories should be transparent to the user – and contributing information. Documents should be captured and managed through a single logical system to maintain a single source of the truth. The emphasis on the business is to amend not the source documents but the records, and act on processes linked to these.

Valuing documents

Value documents for their function, in a process, and content, in decision making.

Two questions should be asked when valuing documents. First, does this document authorise me or instruct me to carry out a task (e.g. purchase order)? Second, does this document provide me with information on which I can check or start a business process? (You might at this stage start to think about the format of your documents.)

View each document type and understand which parts of its content are valuable and to whom. Assess its effectiveness as a document or after transformation into a record.

It should be understood that information needs to be maintained and that not all information is useful. This can reduce the cost of maintenance by reducing the amount of superfluous information.

Categorising documents across all the business

The long-term view should always be taken, prioritising and recording decisions and reasons in the context of the events of today. We can always return to them to reassess their value if appropriate. We should always make sure our systems allow us to do this in a straightforward and a periodic manner. Not enough decision reviews are taken seriously by organisations. These involve routinely asking the same questions, replaying the same scenarios and seeing if the same answers result.

Not everything is solved by electronic documents alone. A balanced view of the future with the resources which are in place at the moment should be maintained. ECM is a method of optimising the business: it is a means, not an end.

Consider the goal. All information should be maintained outside the business at the lowest possible cost over the short, medium and long terms while still retaining its value and compliance to the business. Customers should take and maintain and take responsibility for it so the organisation does not need to employ resources to manage and maintain it.

Standardisation

With the advent of new infrastructures and distributed architectures, some vendors will emphasise the need for standards. However this usually points to promoting a single core generic enterprise platforms standard. Open standards and the use of open source would be a good emphasis.

Total cost of ownership

In times of uncertainty and when there is pressure to achieve better returns on investments, the cost of ownership is forcing heads of IT to reach out for solutions which provide access to scalable resources which can accommodate future growth without increasing their total cost of ownership (TCO). This is a particular problem for ECM which, in the past, has required significant investment in specific hardware: storage disks, optical arrays, backup mechanisms, resilient and highly secure configurations, high throughput multi-page scanners and high-resolution screens.

Adopt whatever scalable mechanisms for resources there are. Ensure that there are alternative sources and fall-back positions for content which becomes too expensive to outsource or maintain.

SUMMARY

We have looked at the business case implementation, the project and the programme. The business case needs to persuade a variety of audiences with an eye on the competitive landscape, manage scope, align to strategic goals and make financial sense.

In programme management ECM is best served by breaking up the project into manageable and deliverable steps. These should concentrate on keeping stakeholders involved, managing and mitigating risks and integrating with key suppliers.

In dealing with the challenges to delivery, there are problems of legacy management, document classification and valuation, as well as in controlling channels of communication and managing change.

12 FUTURE TRENDS

The trouble with our times is that the future is not what it used to be
Paul Valéry

The future of ECM is underpinned by innovations in a number of core technologies. There are a number of technical and conceptual developments which are evolving and changing the landscape in which ECM. To some extent all fundamental information management systems are changing.

In the sphere of management there are collaborative and mobile applications. However with content there will be a fundamental shift to structured documents which encompass semantics and topic construction. Finally the increasingly distributed, enterprise-oriented and universal nature of technology will allow cloud computing to become fully established. These innovations distinguish themselves from those promoted by the marketing campaigns of technology suppliers in that they are transformational, disruptive and universal.

COLLABORATIVE TECHNOLOGIES

Facebook and Twitter, like email in the mid-1990s, have become popular media for communication. It is not necessarily the communication itself which is of interest to businesses and organisations, but the methods by which communication is encouraged, controlled and distributed.

These sophisticated applications provide a complex control of participation amongst the audience. The capabilities of these have an order of magnitude the Simple Mail Transport Protocol (SMTP) which provides the basis for email.

When these technologies become part of the internet, distributed and not centrally controlled, the long-awaited transformation of email will be complete. We will see anonymous address book controls to remove spam, follow-me groups and clearer privacy controls to ensure only agreed information can be revealed.

These applications motivate constructive and structured use, with few rules but the simple etiquette that is established in social groups. These rules already exist in business but are not formalised. Businesses will need to find and embrace an application which allows businesspeople to be motivated to exchange ideas and thoughts, and collaborate.

ECM already uses email as a means to capture the interaction and exchange of ideas. ECM will expand to understand the address space of communication, meaning that the strength of the message, its recipient or recipients and responses to it can be gauged, rather than just its content. Therefore ECM recognises that it is not just the message, but the platform whereby, the time at which and the recipient or recipients to whom it is delivered which make the message significant.

SEMANTIC STRUCTURES

Since the OASIS ratification in 2007 of the DITA V1.1 structured document framework into the technical community, there has been a steady growth in authors moving to XML-based intelligent authoring tools. These enable clearer semantic tagging and topic construction so that authors can organise and manage content without considering a publication format. Word-processing applications such as Microsoft Word will start to reveal and use these hidden templates and methods so that authors and writers can better capture their thoughts and deliberations.

In turn ECM systems will recognise the encapsulated content, stepping beyond the current lowest common denominator of the document. The preserve of web content management (WCM), that of managing snippets of content, will start to be very much a part of ECM.

ATTRIBUTE ACQUISITION

Much work has been done on search technologies, and in aligning them to the concepts of business intelligence through specialist dashboards and similar tools.

A return to the start of the ECM process will result in the development of a natural approach to indexing or cataloguing information that is more than free-form text or a pop-down list of options. There are limitations to the use of pop-down lists: it presupposes that the set of possible attributes is known and predefined, which it rarely is. There are limitations to free form attributes: they make it impossible to retain consistency with other attributes without substantial governance and information management work.

These two challenges can be met by providing smart form acquisition of elements that emerge or organically acquire the values of attributes as the organisation evolves with the ECM system. This will require a departure from the use of pop-down lists and free-form boxes. It will bring in new two-dimensional representations, or word clouds, maps or rings, which allow users to dynamically select or home in on appropriate words to describe their attribute, without necessarily repeating or duplicating words or titles which already exist.

Stephen Fry's recent electronic book is an excellent example of the use of a metadata interface allowing people to read a book non-linearly following associative rather than sequential threads.

BUSINESS INTELLIGENCE

The business intelligence community has focused on the commoditised and stable environment of the structured databases, using data cubes and marts. It will use similar business intelligence techniques with unstructured data. These allow data and dimensions mining. In the new order of content management the dimensions will be perspectives, very much like De Bono's six hats principle.

CLOUD COMPUTING AND SAAS

The market in cloud computing will continue to consolidate. Small innovative companies will promote point technologies, media signature analysis and distributed control.

Cheap pervasive technologies which pretend to do content management have one key issue: to become universal they have to please people most of the time. It is in the nature of ECM that no matter how easy we make our content management to work with, it still requires a fundamental shift in working practices, which many organisations are ill-prepared to countenance. Without a fundamental change in staff mentality or stakeholders' understanding of why they are being asked to index and manage content through the ECM initiative, there is little incentive to use it.

Blogs, wikis and mash-ups are components and structures now being used as viable content which can be managed.

There will be a solid emergence of new skills in records management, ECM architects, librarians and information architects. As part of a collaborative culture, business process management will extend the context of working in varying levels of established and organically growing groups.

ECM technologies will become part of the infrastructure and become commoditised. The search engines will morph into business intelligence tools, with unstructured content still very separate from numerical and structured data.

13 BIBLIOGRAPHY

BOOKS

Boiko, B. (2005) *Content management bible.* John Wiley & Sons, New York, USA.

Chapman, A. M. (2007) *Never talk when you can nod: compliance, ediscovery and enterprise content management systems.* Andrew M. Chapman, NJ, USA.

Davis, J., Miller, G. J. and Russell, A. (2006) *Information revolution: using the information evolution model to grow your business.* John Wiley & Sons, Hoboken, NJ, USA.

Groff, T. R. and Jones, T. P. (2004) *FileNet: a consultant's guide to enterprise content management.* Elsevier Butterworth-Heinemann, Oxford, UK.

Jenkins, T. (2004) *Enterprise content management: technology.* Open Text Corporation, Waterloo, Canada.

McGovern, J., Ambler, S. W., Stevens, M. E., Linn, J., Sharan, V. and Jo, E. K. (2004) *A practical guide to enterprise architecture.* Prentice Hall Professional Technical Reference, Upper Saddle River, NJ, USA.

Patel, P. and McCarthy, M. P. (2000) *Digital transformation: the essentials of e-business leadership.* McGraw-Hill, New York, USA.

Rockley, A., Kostur, P. and Manning, S. (2003) *Managing enterprise content: a unified content strategy.* New Riders, Berkeley, CA, USA.

Szemplinski, P. E. (2009) *ECM buyer beware: real insights and answers for decision makers.* CAPSYS, Colorado Springs, CO, USA.

ARTICLES

Adcock, C. (2007) 'Under control: best practices for document control'. *AIIM E-DOC Magazine*, 21 (3), 42–45.

Adobe Systems (2003) 'Gathering intelligence: the secret of information management'. Executive briefing document.

AIIM (2007) '12 steps to ECM success: best practice for implementing ECM'.

AIIM (2002) 'Content management: managing the lifecycle of information'. AIIM industry white paper on records, document and enterprise content management for the public sector.

Biffar, J. (2010) 'Cloud cover: docuware strategy'. *Document Manager*, 18 (3), 34.

Bird, J. (2011) 'People power'. *Doc. Man.*, 19 (1), 30–31.

Blaik, C. (2009) 'Lowering TCO while managing more content'. *Doc. Man.*, 17 (3), 15–16.

Brookbanks, M. (2010) 'More clouds coming'. *ITNOW*, 53 (3), 16–17.

Brooks, C. (2007) 'Records management 101'. *AIIM E. Mag.*, 21 (3), 16–18.

Burnett, R. (2010) 'Software licences'. *ITNOW*, 52 (4), 24.

Butcher, A. (2009) 'Is it safe?' *Doc. Man.*,17 (1), 24–25.

Carney, A. (2010) 'Five good reasons to automate your AP processes'. *Doc. Man.*, 18 (6), 30.

Chester, B. (2007) 'Information lifecycle'. *AIIM E. Mag.*, 21 (3), 14.

Craddock, P. (2010) 'Cracking the desktop'. *ITNOW*, 52 (4), 6–9.

Davies, M. (2010) 'Turning document templates into information assets'. *Doc. Man.*, 18 (6), 29.

DeSilva, G. and Vednere, G. (2007) 'Lessons from the trenches'. *AIIM E. Mag.*, 21 (6), 26–29.

Duffy, K. (2007) 'XML-based content management: control is king'. *AIIM E. Mag.*, 21 (3), 48–49.

Duhon, B. (2007) 'ECM projects: getting started'. *AIIM E. Mag.*, 21 (3), 58–60.

Duhon, B. (2007) 'A legal look: records from a lawyer's point of view'. *AIIM E. Mag.*, 21 (6), 54–56.

Edwards, C. (2010) 'Sharing what we know'. *Engineering & Technology*, 5 (16), 16–18.

Edwards, C. (2010) 'Semantic web's hidden meanings'. *Eng. & Tech.*, 5 (16), 52–53.

Edwards, C. (2010) 'Forever blowing bubbles'. *Eng. & Tech.*, 5 (16), 70–71.

Ellis, S. (2010) 'The right combination'. *Doc. Man.*, 18 (6), 34.

Ellis, S. (2011) 'Can records managers work in the cloud?' *Doc. Man.*, 19 (1), 22–23.

Fanning, B. (2007) 'Standards to manage electronic records'. *AIIM E. Mag.*, 21 (6), 60–61.

Fanning, B. (2007) 'PDF standards'. *AIIM E. Mag.*, 21 (4), 58–59.

Field, P. (2010) 'Get more from the cloud'. *ITNOW*, 52 (3), 18–19.

Frappaolo, C. (2007) 'Creating corporate DNA through ECM'. *AIIM E. Mag.*, 21 (6), 8–10.

Frear, H. (2010) 'Fleet of foot, and now smarter too'. *Doc. Man.*, 18 (4), 28–29.

Frear, H. (2010) 'Heavy loads ahead'. *Doc. Man.*, 18 (6), 8–9.

Gentile, B. (2010) 'Out of the blocks'. *ITNOW*, 52 (4), 14–15.

Greatorex, M. (2009) 'Focusing on the I in IT'. *Doc. Man.*, 17 (2), 18.

Green, J. (2010) 'Four golden rules for governance'. *Doc. Man.* 18 (5), 20–21.

Harney, J (2007) 'The drive to email archive'. *AIIM E. Mag.*, 21 (6), 32–34.

Harney, J. (2007) 'The consolidation of collaboration'. *AIIM E. Mag.*, 21 (4), 30–38.

Harris, S. (2010) 'Best of both worlds'. *ITNOW*, 52 (4), 16–17.

Hayes, J. (2010) 'Virtual impacts'. *Eng. & Tech.* 5 (13), 54–55.

Hunter, P. (2011) 'Cloud crowd'. *Eng. & Tech.*, 6 (3), 88–89.

IBM (2008) 'The new information agenda: do you have one?'

Intellect (2007) 'Document management concerns the whole board: a guide for all directors'.

Jedd, M. (2007) 'Declaring records'. *AIIM E. Mag.*, 21 (6), 38–41.

Jedd, M. (2007) 'Collaboration tools bring across the board ROI'. *AIIM E. Mag.*, 21 (4), 49–51.

Julien, J. (2007) 'Managing the flow'. *AIIM E. Mag.*, 21 (6), 12–18.

Julien, J. (2007) 'Championing email management: how to convince end users to buy into email management'. *AIIM E. Mag.*, 21 (3), 29–30.

Kass, S. (2007) 'How to propose: why do we need a project proposal?' *AIIM E. Mag.*, 21 (3), 12.

Levin, R. (2007) 'Digital signatures: coming soon to a document near you'. *AIIM E. Mag.*, 21 (6), 24–25.

Lloyd, G. (2007) 'Blogs and wikis: building customer connections'. *AIIM E. Mag.*, 21 (4), 42–44.

Lin, E. and Haas, L. (2002) 'IBM federated database technology'.

Lin, S. (2010) 'Performance enhancing DM'. *Doc. Man.*, 18 (5), 18–19.

Magon, Dr V. (2010) 'Procurement vs partnership: mutually exclusive?' *Doc. Man.*, 18 (6), 12–13.

Magon, Dr V. (2010) 'Authority figures'. *Doc. Man.*, 18 (4), 20–21.

Magon, Dr. V. (2009) 'Compliance on trial'. *Doc. Man.*, 17 (6), 10–12.

Magon, Dr. V. (2009/2010) 'Can eforms help us break the paper habit?' *Doc. Man.*, 17 (3), 26–28 and 18 (2), 24–27.

Mancini, J. (2007) 'Sausage, laws and ECM'. *AIIM E. Mag.*, 21 (3), 6.

Mancini, J. F. (2007) 'Positioning for a flat world'. *AIIM E. Mag.*, 21 (6), 4.

Mannings, R. (2010) 'Towards a parallel world'. *Eng. & Tech.*, 5 (16), 23–25.

Mansperger, M. (2007) '10 Steps to prepare for ediscovery'. *AIIM E. Mag.*, 21 (4), 14–18.

Maurer, S. (2009) 'Speed isn't everything'. *Doc. Man.*, 17 (3), 18–19.

May, T. (2007) 'Privacy looms in your future'. *AIIM E. Mag.*, 21 (4), 63.

May, T. (2007) 'Innovation 101 for those would have a future'. *AIIM E. Mag.*, 21 (3), 63.

May, T. (2007) 'ECM 4.0: mental modeling YOUR future'. *AIIM E. Mag.*, 21 (6), 64.

Medina, R. and Chambers B. (2007) 'Non-technology components of an enterprise records management strategy'. *AIIM E. Mag.*, 21 (3), 23–26.

Miles, D. (2010) 'State of the ECM industry 2010: meeting demands of a new decade'. *Doc. Man.*, 18 (3), 32–33.

Mills, J. (2009) 'Rising to the challenge'. *Doc. Man.*, 17 (1), 14–16.

Pyke, J. (2007) 'Why workflow stinks'. *AIIM E. Mag.*, 21 (4), 64.

Reamy, T. (2007) 'Taxonomy development advice'. *AIIM E. Mag.*, 21 (6), 35–37.

Russell-Rose, T., Kruschwitz, U. and MacFarlane, A. (2011) 'Future searching'. *ITNOW*, 53 (1), 14–15.

Santos-Serrao, P. (2007) 'Does my organisation need document control?' *AIIM E. Mag.*, 21 (3), 50–51.

Scholtes, J. (2007) 'How to make ediscovery and edisclosure easier'. *AIIM E. Mag.*, 21 (4), 24–26.

Scott, J. (2007) 'Storage acquisitions and the future'. *AIIM E. Mag.*, 21 (3), 64.

Shackleton, J. (2009) 'Protect and survive'. *Doc. Man.*, 17 (6), 20–21.

Sharpe, B. (2009) 'Finding the right tool for the job'. *Doc. Man.*, 17 (5), 28–30.

Sinur, J. (2007) 'What's process got to do with it?' *AIIM E. Mag.*, 21 (6), 22–23.

Smith, S. (2010) 'Can open source be secure?' *ITNOW*, 52 (4), 18–19.

Stephenson, D. (2007) 'Accelerating compliance'. *AIIM E. Mag.*, 21 (4), 27–29.

Stone, C. (2007) 'Email and ediscovery'. *AIIM E. Mag.*, 21 (4), 19–22.

Sutherland, G. (2011) 'Building quality into projects'. *ITNOW*, 53 (1), 30–31.

Swabey, P. (2010) 'Holding IT to account'. *Information Age*, November, 16–18.

Tombs, K. (2008) 'When silos gently collide'. *IQ magazine*, 24 (1), 34–7.

Tominna, M. (2007) 'The 4 ps of collaboration systems: purpose, process, pitch and promotion'. *AIIM E. Mag.*, 21 (4), 39–41.

Twentyman, J. (2010) 'Expense in store'. *Information Age*, November, 21–23.

Tyler, D. (2011) 'Don't pay the penalty'. *Doc. Man.*, 19 (1), 32–34.

Violino B. (2007) 'Collaboration toolbox'. *AIIM E. Mag.*, 21 (4), 45–48.

Wang, A. (2010) 'Balance of power'. *Doc. Man.*, 18 (6), 28.

Watson, J., Patel, J., Desai, G. and Chambers B. (2007) 'ECM in 2008: compliance takes centre stage'. *AIIM E. Mag.*, 21 (6), 42–45.

Weideman, R. (2010) 'Best of both worlds: distributed centralised scanning'. *Doc. Man.*, 18 (3), 24–25.

Weigl, M. (2010) 'Enterprise approach to capture: developing the compelling business case'. *Doc. Man.*, 18 (3), 15–17.

Weise, C. (2007) 'Eliminate records clutter'. *AIIM E. Mag.*, 21 (3), 19–23.

Wilkins, J. (2007) 'Web 2.0 what does it mean and why does it matter?' *AIIM E. Mag.*, 21 (4), 10–11.

INTERNET REFERENCES

AIIM (the association for information and image management). (www.aiim.org)

AIIM Communities (formerly AIIM eDoc and Infonomics magazine). (www.aiimcommunities.org)

Darwin Information Typing Architecture (DITA XML). (xml.coverpages.org/dita.html)

ECM Connection (ECM Technology and Practices). (www.ecmconnection.com)

ECM Guide (the complementary site to this book that is specific to product, suppliers and innovation news). (www.ecmguide.org)

Intellect (UK Technology Industry). (www.intellectuk.org)

MIKE2.0 (open source standard for information management). (mike2.openmethodology.org)

MoReq: Model Requirements for Management of Electronic Records. (www.moreq.info)

Real story group (content management technology analysis). (www.realstorygroup.com)

Southbeach (modelling risk/benefit tool). (www.southbeachinc.com)

OFFICIAL PUBLICATIONS

United States–Vietnam Relations, 1945–1967: A Study Prepared by the Department of Defense (1969) Arlington County, VA: USDOD

INDEX